# OF DAYS
# GONE BY

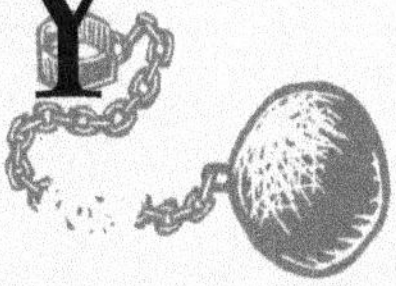

# OF DAYS GONE BY

Richard A. Henry

**ARPress**
ILLUMINATING IDEAS.
EMPOWERING VOICES

**ARPress LLC**
45 Dan Road Suite 5
Canton MA 02021
Hotline: 1(888) 821-0229
Fax:      1(508) 545-7580

Ordering Information:
Quantity sales. Special discounts are available on quantity purchases by corporations, associations, and others. For details, contact the publisher at the address above.

Printed in the United States of America.

ISBN-13:    Softcover       979-8-89330-259-2
            Hardcover       979-8-89330-260-8
            eBook           979-8-89330-258-5

Library of Congress Control Number:    2024901502

# TABLE OF CONTENTS

I wish to express my thanks to my friend
and ex-wife, Genée D. Jackson-Henry.
It is largely because of her love, friendship,
encouragement, editing skills,
and faith in my abilities that my dreams
of writing Of Days Gone By
became reality. Thanks, Genee!

I also dedicate this edition in memory of:

My Father,
Junius Stergus Henry
May 1, 1925 – April 1, 1997

My Mother
Nancy Elizebeth Venters

My Grandmother,
Ethel P. Forrest

My Grandmother
Helena Jan Henry

This book is also dedicated to the memory of:

Tecklen

Jeanette

Jarriot Staten

Elisha Cromwell

Nancy Ann Staten;

Joseph Venters

Clarise Buck

John Wilson

Shadric Richard Venters

Nancy Elizabeth Wilson

William Leander Lane

Penina Cromwell Staten

George Venters

Clara (Venters) Hardy

Chester Venters

Golden Thomas Venters

Robert Venters

Thedora Lane

Simone Lane

Ethel Lane-Forrest

Helena Jan Henry

Golden Thomas Venters II

And all the members of my family
who have preceded me in life and death.
Without their having been,
I would not be.

I also dedicate this book to my dear Friend,
Janice Elaine Pittman,
Who Left for A Happier Place On,
April 6, 2003

Grandfather, or Pop, as those who knew him well affectionately called him, was born a free man on Easter Sunday, in 1841. Except for his time in the Army and the first eighteen years of his life, which he spent on his father's farm on Long Island, Pop resided in New York City. Now almost eighty-eight years to the day, he was laid out in his burial clothes, a few short hours away from being covered by the soil he had loved so much.

I arrived at St. Philip's Protestant Episcopal Church an hour before the funeral services, for I wanted to spend a few last moments alone with him. Although I could no longer be blessed with his physical presence, I would always have his spiritual companionship and the richness of the many stories he had shared with me.

Until a few weeks ago, when Pop became too weak to speak for long periods, I delighted in listening to the countless stories he loved to tell. I never knew his wife, my grandmother. She passed away when my father, their son and only child, was in his early teens.

Unfortunately, I never got to know my father either. He was murdered one night while on his way home from visiting a few friends over in Black Bohemia, a name given to the neighborhood situated on the west side of Manhattan, between Twenty-seventh and Fifty-third streets. At the turn of the century, it was the center of the Negro section of New York City. The police claimed that my father was a victim of a mugger. As far as they were concerned, the case was closed. After all it was just another "nigger killing."

My mother never did get over my father's sudden and unexpected death. She was an orphan with no knowledge of her roots. The home she and my father had shared the five years prior to his death was the first and only place she had been able to call her own. One day, shortly after receiving the news of my father's death, she took me over to Pop's house and asked him if he would watch me for a couple of hours. She was never heard from, nor seen again. I was four years old at the time, and all I can remember about my mother was that, as most mothers appear to their children, she was the most beautiful woman in the world.

The first time I questioned Pop about why my mother just left me and went away, he gave me a straightforward, honest reply.

"I can't answer that. No one knows what goes through a person's mind when they decide to do something. I do know that your mother loved you very much. Whatever her reason was for leaving you with me, I know that it hurt her very much to do it."

"Will you ever leave me, Grandpop?" I asked tearfully.

I remember almost as if it just happened yesterday how Pop picked me up, gently placed me on his lap and looked at me for a good minute. At first, I was scared by what I saw as I looked past his thick, greying eyebrows and eyelashes into his deep-set, brown tear-filled eyes. When I listened to his answer, I found a peace I would experience time and time again during the next two and a half decades, whenever I was troubled and needed comfort. "No, I'll never leave you," he promised. Then he wiped away a single tear that had begun to make its way down his cheek and gave me a hug. His gentle, yet firm embrace made me feel as if a force of inner strength had been transmitted from him to me.

Somehow, I expected him to live forever. I never once gave any thought to his dying. He was always so full of energy and seemed to live life to the fullest, despite the times in which he lived. I was taken completely by surprise a few weeks ago when, without warning, he fell victim to a stroke. Pop wouldn't let me check him into the hospital, as his doctor had advised.

"I've lived a full and happy life. I'm not going to die in some cold hospital room, especially not in "The Morgue." My home is filled with good memories and warm feelings. Here is where I'll leave this world."

My arguments with Pop, to let me take him to the hospital where he could receive proper care, were pointless. He let me know that the only thing he wanted or needed was the feeling of security and love that was abundant in his home.

It was useless to continue pushing the point with Pop. After I thought about it for a while, I decided he was right. He was more secure and probably safer at home, in the long run, than he would be at the Morgue."

"The Morgue" or the "Butcher Shop" were just two of the names local residents gave to Harlem Hospital. Not only was it the only hospital serving a community whose population density per acre, in 1929, was nearly twice that of the rest of the city, but it was the only one in the city that admitted

Negroes. Negroes in other parts of the city, who sought admission to hospitals near their homes, were rerouted to Harlem Hospital for medical care.

Pop had constantly used his influence and wealth to try and get the administration at Harlem Hospital to hire more Negro doctors and nurses. In 1927, out of a staff of more than fifty doctors at the facility, only seven were Negro.

"It isn't because there aren't enough Negro physicians around. The latest figures show that there are more than three hundred in the city," Pop argued.

Pop's wealth and influence as a businessman could have gotten him into a small private hospital, but he wouldn't hear of it. He passed away peacefully four days ago, with me by his side.

It was three in the afternoon when I quietly entered Pop's room to see if he was resting comfortably. Somehow, he had managed to prop himself up in bed. When he saw me, he smiled and motioned for me to sit on the bed next to him. He didn't say a word. Instead, he gave me a big, warm smile and extended his loving hand. It was a source of comfort to me. I inquired how he was feeling. "At peace," was the last thing he said before he closed his eyes and breathed his last breath.

Unknown to me, Pop had anticipated his death. As was his style, he had left nothing to chance. He had prearranged every detail of his funeral and burial. His last wishes were clearly spelled out in a letter addressed to me. I found it tucked securely between the pages of the Bible he kept under his pillow during his last few days on earth.

Uncle Sam had drafted the letter. Sam wasn't actually a blood relative, but he had been much more than just Pop's best friend for the past fifty years. He had also been his attorney and partner in several business endeavors throughout the years. Despite his partial paralysis from the stroke, Pop managed to sign the letter. As always, his signature was crystal clear with bold looping letters. He took great pride in his name and used every occasion, which called for his signature, to express that pride.

As I sat in silence, looking lovingly at Pop laying in his silk lined casket, I thought back to a few of the many fond memories he had left with me. He was a gifted storyteller. Whenever he shared bits of his past with me through his many stories, it seemed as if I was transported back through the barriers of time, and living the events he so skillfully related.

Most of his storytelling took place on the stoop of the brownstone, which he owned, and we lived in. It was on West Twenty-seventh Street between Seventh and Eighth Avenues. At the turn of the century, we were one of only two Negro families living on the block.

Pop's house was the best-kept brownstone on the street. In front of the house there was a large, very old oak tree. A three-foot high, wrought iron fence placed there to protect it from the dogs that freely roamed the neighborhood surrounded the little patch of dirt at the base of the tree. An identical fence surrounded the front of the house. Just inside was a black cast iron bench and two matching chairs. The house had several entrances. One could enter through the street-level door under the steps, which was guarded by a steel gate, or you could climb the fourteen wide brick steps that led to the second floor entrance.

The rooms inside were spacious, with fourteen-foot ceilings and large windows that let in an abundance of daylight. The stairs in the house were made of solid oak, as were the window frames, the long beams that stretched across the ceilings in each room, and the baseboards that wrapped around the edge of the floors. The interior doors were constructed from handcrafted mahogany. There were several sets of massive sliding doors that separated some of the rooms on the second floor. All the wood in the house was kept highly polished.

Everything in the house seemed to have a place, and everything was always in its place. Each spacious room was tastefully decorated and comfortably furnished. A variety of colorful area rugs adorned the wooden floors, and several of the rooms had fireplaces.

Pop was rather well off. Besides having inherited a considerable amount of New York City real estate and a rather large sum of cash from his father, Pop had added substantial holdings to his estate portfolio from his various business enterprises throughout the years. Even if he hadn't made a penny from any of his businesses, he could have lived comfortably off his inheritance.

In his younger days, Pop entertained quite lavishly. When one of his friends dropped in, he instructed the housekeeper to set out the finest China and insisted that his guest stay for supper. Back then, Helen was his housekeeper. She never fussed about an extra guest or two, regardless of how unexpected they were. Helen had been Pop's housekeeper for many years before I came to live with him. Actually, she was more like a member of the family than an employee.

Uncle Sam was Pop's oldest and dearest friend. Like clockwork, every Saturday promptly at five, as far back as I can remember, he arrived at the house with a box of pastry in one hand and two hand-rolled Cuban cigars in the other.

He'd enter and greet us, then give me the box of pastry, and hand one of the cigars to Pop. I usually headed into the kitchen, where I hurriedly opened the box of goodies, anxious to see what was inside.

In the interim, weather permitting, Pop and Sam would retreat to the stoop, where they sat on the top step, facing each other, backs pressed against the wall, and lit their cigars. I'd soon join them, with a piece of fresh pastry in hand, and find them sitting in silence.

The pleasure they derived from the cigars seemed to increase with each puff. I would sit in the middle, alternating glances back and forth between them. They delighted me by blowing smoke rings from the large cigars clasped firmly between their teeth. Silently, they competed with each other, each in turn trying to make a larger ring of smoke or get more rings from a single mouthful of smoke than the other. This went on until the last puff that could be drawn from their cigars had been extracted.

Once they savored the last bit of smoke and put out their cigars, they would simultaneously look directly at me for my decision as to who had performed the best. I never answered verbally. Instead, I just pointed to the victor and smiled. After my vote was in, the winner would look at the loser and wink. The two of them would then exchange friendly smiles. Once the ritual was completed, the three of us would sit in silence, gazing at the folks strolling up and down Eighth Avenue.

The silence was broken from time to time by the greeting of a passing neighbor. "Good afternoon, gentlemen. How are you this fine day?"

"Fine, just fine," the two of them would respond, almost echoing one another.

Occasionally, someone would stop just outside the gate for an extended chat. This went on for a good half-hour or so, until Helen's familiar voice summoned us to supper.

How Helen came to work for Pop is, in itself, an interesting story. She was about the same age as he, and a few years older than Uncle Sam. Unlike them, she had her roots in the South and was born a slave. During slavery, she was bred to be what was then called a "house nigger," or more specifically, a cook. She was as fortunate as anyone born a slave could be, because as a child, she was never separated from her mother and father. Her mother was in charge of all the other house niggers on the plantation, which was located a few miles outside of Charleston, South Carolina.

Helen lived and labored on the same plantation until the end of the Civil War. Her father had also worked in the big house until just prior to the war, when he was sold to a plantation owner from Alabama.

According to her own account, from the time that she was able to walk and talk, she followed her mother around the house, while learning what was expected of her. She spent her adolescent years mastering sewing and cooking for the master and his family. She considered herself lucky to have been born a slave to what she described as a caring and kind master.

The family who owned her had two girls close to her own age. When she was very young, they befriended her and delighted in teaching her to read, write and count. Of course, soon after she reached her teen years, the innocence of childhood passed and the reality of the times set in. She was, after all, a slave, and her childhood friends were the master's children. As she grew older she learned what that meant, and so did they.

Although Helen told us that she had never been whipped, she had seen the lash put to a few other slaves, and what she saw left its mark. She did a very thorough job of conveying a vivid picture of what a slave whipping was like. I shook and cringed the first time she told me. She reverted to her southern accent, which she always did when she spoke of her days as a slave.

"Whenever a slave wuz going to be whipped, we wuz all gathered out in front of the barn and made to watch. The master, in his thinking, figured that by us seeing a whipping, we would learn to be good niggers and not give him what he considered just cause for a whipping. But listen to me when I tell you, there ain't no just cause to whip a person likes I seen them mean white folks whip a body.

"The master never whipped none of us personally or stood around to watch. He didn't have the stomach for it. But Missah John, he delighted in putting the lash against a man's skin. Usually, it was one of the field hands. Missah John wuz the overseer, and it didn't take much wrongdoing for him to decide a good whipping wuz what a body needed to keep him in place.

"Well anyway, we wuz all gathered in front of the barn and made to watch. Whoever wuz Missah John's victim, wuz tied to the big oak tree in front of the barn. Tied him good and tight, too, so as to make sure that he couldn't slide down when the lash was put to him. It wuz the most horrible thing to see. Missah John would rear back and, with his face twisted as if he were the devil himself come to earth, swing that long brown bullwhip. With every bit of strength he could muster, he'd set the bullwhip against that poor man's bare back, cutting into the flesh. The loud crack of the whip sounded like thunder in the night.

"Although it wuzn't you who was getting whipped, I swear it wuz as if you felt each lash. There wuzn't any set number of lashes he would give, either. Missah John would swing that whip again and again, with each lash tearing away more and more flesh, until either his victim passed out from the pain, or until there wuzn't an unwhipped spot or any skin left on his back. Then he'd cut him loose and tell the other field hands to get him out of there. Missah John always expected whoever it wuz that he had just torn the flesh off of to be back in the field with all the other niggers at first light."

After the war, Helen moved to Charleston proper and stayed for twenty years. She was luckier than most of the newly freed slaves. She was a skilled seamstress and an excellent cook. Her mother stayed on at the old plantation, working for their former master. Helen never married and after her mother passed away, there was nothing to keep her in the South. She had heard good things about the North, and she wanted to escape the painful reminders of her slave days, which were all around her.

It was 1885 when Helen finally arrived in New York City. She had a sister who had married one of the colored troopers serving with the Massachusetts Fifty-fourth, and she had joined him in New York after the war ended.

Pop was also a veteran of the Fifty-fourth and a close friend of Helen's brother-in-law. Pop's wife had passed away the year before, and he was looking for a domestic to care for his house and to help care for my father. He was introduced to Helen and made her a generous offer of employment, which she accepted.

For years, Helen maintained her own residence a few blocks from where Pop owned a house at the time, just on the edge of Black Bohemia. When Pop purchased the house on 127th Street, he had the third floor converted into an apartment for her.

In many ways, Helen was Pop's good friend, and he was the same to her. Although neither would ever admit it, I knew that over the years they had come to depend on each other, even though they never became romantically involved.

Helen raised my father because, at the time, Pop was a man about town. When he wasn't working or entertaining at home, he was out being entertained. She was also like a mother to me. By the time I was abandoned at Pop's house by my mother, he had mellowed with age, so he took a more active role in raising me than he had with my father.

Helen died after a bout with pneumonia on June 29, 1915. The date stands out clearly in my mind because it was my fifteenth birthday. Pop was deeply grieved by her passing. She had been a member of the family for almost thirty years.

Her unexpected death left its mark on us. I still miss her to this day. She was an intricate part of my growing up. She used to get as big a kick as I did from listening to Pop's stories.

After supper, Pop, Sam and I would return to the stoop. By then, the sun was nearly gone from the sky or, on many occasions, it had already set. Sam and Pop would each light up another cigar, and slowly puff away without the fanfare that went along with their smoke before supper.

Not long after they were finished enjoying their after-supper smoke, Helen would join us. She was too much of a lady to sit directly on the stoop. She didn't consider it proper. Upon seeing her, I would dash inside and get her sitting chair, a rocker that had belonged to her mother. Other than money saved while working in Charleston, a bag of clothes and the rocker were the only possessions she had brought North.

After I returned with her sitting chair and she was seated comfortably, the three of us would turn toward Pop. Once he was sure he had our undivided attention, he would begin telling us a story, in a delightful mixture of events of the past told to him, and those he had actually experienced. "I never tell a story that I haven't lived or heard about firsthand," he'd remind us.

From the moment he began to speak to the end of the story, I listened with eyes closed, reliving each scene.

Despite my orphanhood, so to speak, my childhood and young adulthood were full of good times, and I have numerous fond memories. The best of those times were spent listening to Pop tell his stories.

# CHAPTER TWO

One of the first stories I remember Pop telling us was his version of how he came to be born in America. It was close to eight-thirty on a warm August evening. The sun had just about set, and things had begun settling down in the neighborhood. The majority of our neighbors had retreated to the confines of their houses, or sat on stoops enjoying a slight breeze that blew away some of the day's heat. While it was pretty quiet on our block, once the sun had set, we could hear a wide variety of noises coming from Eighth and Seventh Avenues as a good number of horse-drawn carriages and wagons made their way down them. Occasionally, a lone rider and his mount galloped past.

There wasn't much traffic in our neighborhood in the latter part of the evening. The automobile or horseless carriage, as it was referred to at that time, was new on the scene and not every horse took kindly to passing automobiles. Lots of folks seemed to delight in seeing the animals spooked. They laughed when a rider was thrown or a horse pulling a carriage or wagon suddenly bolted forward, throwing back the driver and passengers. Such actions were commonplace whenever a passing automobile's engine backfired. For what it was worth, it was part of the free nightly entertainment.

By the time the sun set completely, and the last signs of daylight disappeared from the sky, Pop and Sam had finished smoking their second cigar of the evening and Pop began his story. He opened all his tales, regardless of how much of it was fact or fiction, by saying, "The story I'm about to tell is true, at least as I remember it. I may be getting old, but my memory is still damn good."

Pop looked at each of us in turn to insure, that he had our complete attention, then continued with his narrative. "If how I came to be born in America is going to be clear to you, I have to first tell you a little about a few events which occurred before I was born."

You could see it in Pop's face. When he spoke, he enjoyed every moment of it. He claimed that his grandfather on his mother's side was an African griot (oral historian) and that he had inherited his ability to memorize and pass on history verbally from him. I looked at Pop the first few minutes that he spoke, then leaned back against the steps and shut my eyes. It wasn't long before I was completely captivated by his story, mesmerized, transported back through time, until there I was, living the events that he was so skillfully describing.

"Now don't get me wrong. I'm not excusing the white man or trying to make light of the cruelty of slavery. I'm just trying to give you a clear idea of how easy it was for Europeans to enslave and uproot so many millions of us from our motherland Africa." He continued, "Sure, some Africans were captured and forced into slavery by European slavers, but the majority weren't. You see, when the first Europeans arrived in Africa, sometime between 1441 and 1445, slavery was a part of African life. Inter-tribal warfare was commonplace and to the victor went the spoils.

"The spoils were the survivors of the defeated. The victors enslaved them and took them back to their tribal lands and villages. When the Europeans arrived, African kings and chiefs gladly traded their slaves for brandy, cloth, trinkets, and other goods. The Europeans then transported the slaves to various colonies, where most were forced to work the fields.

"As the farming of sugar cane, tobacco and cotton increased, so did the need for slaves. To help meet this increasing demand, the Europeans encouraged inter-tribal warfare and supplied many of the coastal tribes with sophisticated weapons, with which to defeat inland tribes and provide them with more and more slaves. Once captured, these slaves were kept in factories along the coast until they were loaded onto ships headed for the colonies in the Americas. The factories were forts, called barracoons. Unlike conventional forts though, they weren't heavily fortified. Most protection was provided by the same Africans who brought many of the slaves held captive in the factories.

"Quite often, there were a few white men present at the factories. The white employees were known as factors. They lived at the factory and were looked after by the local chief, who provided them with as many comforts as they wanted, which included African mistresses supplied from the local slave population.

"My mother was a member of the Mandingo tribe, who had been taken captive somewhere up the Senegal River and made a slave. She was given to an Englishman named John Covington, who had a partnership in a slave-trading company and ran a factory along the Gambia River in Mandingo country. My mother was without a doubt the most beautiful woman that ever graced this earth, and it didn't take the Englishman long to fall in love with her. Shortly after she was given to the Englishman, he got rid of his other mistresses and kept my mother as his only companion. They lived together for two years, within the confines of the factory.

"In 1838, the Englishman, for reasons known only to him, decided to abandon the slave-trading business and settle in America. He took my mother with him and set sail for the United States, arriving in New York harbor in the latter part of '38.

"The Englishman had amassed a fortune during his years as a part of the flourishing slave-trading business. He purchased several tracts of land on Long Island, and he employed people to manage and work his farm while he set about purchasing real estate in New York City proper. Although he saw to it that her every need was met, the Englishman kept my mother tucked safely away out on Long Island. To make a long story somewhat shorter, in October of '40 he impregnated her without the benefit of marriage, and I was born the following June.

"My mother, with help from the Englishman, learned to read and write English quite well by the time I had been conceived.

"In 1839, an incident occurred which captivated my mother. Some fifty Africans, aboard a slave ship name the L'Amistad; had been purchased by two Spaniards in Cuba. While waiting shipment to Principe, they rose up in the night, seized several weapons from the sleeping sailors, killed the ship's captain and cook, then strapped the two men who had purchased them to the bridge and ordered them to guide the ship back to Africa.

"The leader of the shipboard rebellion, or mutiny, as the press referred to it, was named Joseph Cinque, a name obviously given him by the press, for I seriously doubt that was his African name. Instead of steering the ship southwest toward Africa, the two Spaniards would steer the ship northeast, during the night. After sailing for sixty-three days, the L'Amistad landed off the coast of Long Island and was boarded by the United States Navy. As one can imagine, the boarding party was quite surprised at what they discovered.

"The Africans were arrested and charged with murder before the United States Circuit Court at New Haven. The newspapers provided continuous coverage of the incident, from the time the L'Amistad landed on Long Island right up until and through the trial. Cinque and his fellow Africans' case was argued before the U.S. Supreme Court by John Quincy Adams, a staunch abolitionist.

"Adams made a brilliant defense, and on March 9, 1841, the Supreme Court ordered Cinque and the other Africans to be freed. My mother was proud of Cinque and considered him a true hero. When I was born in June of that year, she named me after Joseph Cinque. My birth came at great cost, for my mother died giving me life."

At that point in his story, Pop paused for a long moment. I opened my eyes and looked at him in time to see him wipe away a tear rolling down his cheek. While I studied him, I realized that he had never referred to the Englishman as his father; only "The Englishman." I closed my eyes again as he continued his story.

"My mother must have been truly fascinated by the story of the L'Amistad and its crew. She kept a scrapbook full of newspaper accounts of the entire affair. One day, when I was, oh I guess I must have been ten or eleven, I was playing in the attic when I discovered a large steamer trunk. Like any normal boy that age, I let my imagination run wild. I quickly ran over to the ladder, which I had climbed to get in the attic, and grabbed the lantern. Holding it at arm's length, I slowly made my way back to the trunk. As I crept toward it, I imagined that I was slowly inching my way through a darkened cave, searching for hidden treasures. When I reached the trunk, I carefully placed the lantern on the floor next to my discovery. At last, I had found the hidden treasure. Slowly I opened the lid, preparing to step back from the blinding light of gold coins, diamonds, rubies, and emeralds that were certainly inside.

"Now under most circumstances, my vivid imagination would have allowed me to momentarily see the stolen pirate treasures inside my find. But when I threw back the lid, I immediately recognized that the trunk was full of a woman's old clothing. It didn't take me longer than a second or two to guess that the clothes I had found were my mother's. You see, the Englishman never could bring himself to talk much about her. Whenever I questioned him, he would only tell me that she was the most beautiful woman in the world and that he had loved her very much. Well, I wasted no time in digging through the trunk, hoping to find out more about my mother from her belongings.

Within a few minutes, I realized that I had indeed chanced upon a treasure. Beneath the clothing were several scrapbooks full of newspaper clippings and drawings of events that must have been of interest to her.

"Most were about issues dealing with slavery: runaway slaves, anti-slavery, free Negroes, and stories of numerous different slave rebellions.

"I was startled to discover that a rebellion of slaves and indentured servants had been planned in Gloucester County, Virginia, in 1663, and that closer to home, in 1712, rebellious slaves in New York had killed several white men. There was an article giving the details of Gabriel's planned attack on Richmond, how he was betrayed and subsequently hanged in 1800.

"Still another described how Danmark Vesey, a free Negro, planned one of the largest revolts ever recorded. He, too, was betrayed in 1822.

"Included were several articles about Nat Turner's revolt in Virginia in 1831. Before the rebellion was quelled, Nat Turner and his band of rebels had slain more than sixty white people."

"I continued flipping through the scrapbooks realizing for the first time that the Negro in America had a rich and colorful past.

"How long I stayed in the attic flipping through those scrapbooks escapes my memory at the moment, but I still recall one article I read several times. Each time, I grew angrier and angrier. It was an article describing the trip and conditions African slaves had endured during their long voyage to America.

"The trip was referred to in the article, as the 'Middle Passage.' It explained that Middle Passage was a term used to describe the sea lane which the slave ships followed across the Atlantic to the Americas. The article presented a vivid description of the conditions aboard the average slave ship. Male and female slaves were stowed in separate compartments beneath the top deck of the ship. In most cases the slaves are stacked like logs inches apart, in small cramped holes. They are always shackled together. Each day, weather permitting, they are brought up on deck, hosed down and kept above deck for a few minutes of fresh air and exercise. Whenever the opportunity presents itself, slaves throw themselves overboard. Many slaves prefer being eaten by sharks to being taken alive to a strange land. There are several buckets set about, in the slave compartments, for them to relieve themselves. Yet, on many occasions, the manner in which they are bound together, coupled with the total void of space in which to move about, makes any attempt to reach the buckets useless. As a result, human waste literally covers the planks on which the slaves are stowed. It is not uncommon for the captain and members of the ship's crew to take whatever liberties they feel like taking with the female slaves.'

"I also found an old announcement from a South Carolina newspaper describing a slave auction. It read, in part, 'A credit sale of a prime gang of fifty-two cotton Negroes will take place on Tuesday at one o'clock at the Jeffer's plantation.' The advertisement went on to describe several of the slaves, by age and the general condition of their health. If they were skilled in any way, that was also listed. The advertisement concluded by announcing that, 'the Negroes for sale could be inspected two days prior to said sale.'

"Finally, after I had read or flipped through the scrapbooks several times, I closed them and returned them to the trunk. After carefully placing my mother's clothing back on top of the books, I shut it. I remained in the attic, trying to absorb and make sense out of all that I had just read.

"Playing in the attic had been forbidden, so I dared not share my find with anyone. After what must have been hours, I carefully made my way back down the ladder and snuck out of the house. There was a stream a few hundred yards from the back of the house where I would go whenever I was troubled and wanted to think. I would try to work out whatever was troubling me in the quiet tranquility that the gentle flowing waters of the stream surrounded me with. A lot of what I had just seen and read left me troubled, so I headed for the stream.

"After my mother's death, the Englishman spent most of his time in New York City. I was left in the care of several servants. The Englishman would return to the farm at least once a month and on most holidays. Although it was common knowledge that I was his son and he was my father, the Englishman never addressed me as 'Son,' and I always addressed him as 'Sir.' Whenever the Englishman was home, conversation between us was always polite. It was clear, even to me in my youth, that he was a deeply troubled man.

"The Englishman provided me with private tutors, who came out to the farm several days a week. My education continued in this manner until my seventeenth birthday. The benefit of several good private teachers provided me with an excellent education. The Englishman saw to it that I wanted for nothing, materially. Yet emotionally, I felt deprived and robbed. An angry fire raged inside of me.

"George, a free Negro in his mid-fifties, was in charge of things when the Englishman was away. He always sent one of the servants into the village for the newspaper. When he was through reading and had discarded it, I retrieved it from the trash and looked for articles to add to the collection my mother had begun. Often, I returned to the attic and re-read the articles contained in the scrapbooks. How my mother managed to collect all the newspaper clippings still remains a mystery to me. Some of them were dated long before she arrived in America or was even born.

"Many of the articles that I added to the collection were clipped from several newspapers the Englishman brought with him when he returned to the farm. George always seemed as if he couldn't wait for the Englishman to return and pass on copies of a Negro newspaper named Freedom's Journal. He would also bring copies of Garrisson's Liberator and a local New York paper, The Emancipator.

"Included with these newspapers, which all directed themselves toward the elimination of slavery and the rights or lack of rights of Negroes, there were always several copies of The Tribune. Its editor, Horace Greeley, was a strong supporter of 'The Negro Cause.'

"It was when I began reading these papers and understanding what they were about that I first began to suspect that the Englishman was tending to more than just real estate when he was in New York City.

"For the next several years, I continued to add to the collection of clippings that my mother had started. I did this from the newspapers George read almost daily, and from the ones the Englishman brought to the farm.

"I had to be quick about clipping articles from the latter group of papers. Whenever George was through reading them, he would fold them up and toss them into the fireplace to be burnt later in the day. When the opportunity presented itself, I would sneak into the parlor and hastily clip out as many articles as I could. When I was done, I would re-fold the papers, careful to hide any signs that they had been tampered with, and place the now mutilated papers back into the fireplace in the same spot where they had landed earlier. This went on for several years.

"Discovering the trunk in the attic, and availing myself of the wealth of information contained in the scrapbooks, made me increasingly aware that there were a lot of things the Englishman was keeping secret from me.

"When I was fourteen, I began to notice that there was something strange about the manner in which the Englishman conducted himself. The fact that he always returned home during the night while I slept began to disturb me.

"When he was home, the cook seemed to prepare more food than we could consume. For a while, I figured she was cooking extra for the other servants and farm workers. That served as a good explanation, until I noticed that there was always smoke emitting from the chimneys of the servants' and the workers' quarters around mealtime, a clear indication they were cooking for themselves. Yet, the day after the Englishman returned home and the abundance of food had been prepared, it seemed to simply disappear.

"For the likes of me, I couldn't figure out what was happening to the food. I suppose I could have simply confronted the Englishman, George, or the cook, but I was quite curious by nature and had long ago resolved to find out what the Englishman was all about. The disappearing food was just another piece in the puzzle which I was determined to piece together without anyone else's help."

It was at this point in the story that Sam interrupted. "Well, Joseph, I hate to be the spoilsport, but it's getting late and I had best be getting home."

Like so many other things between Sam and Pop, his departure took on the form of a ritual. Helen and I amused ourselves by synchronizing our lips with theirs and silently speaking along with them. Helen imitated Sam and I imitated Pop. "You're welcome to spend the night, Sam."

"Wish that I could Joseph, but there are things I have to do in the morning."

"Now what things have you got to do in the morning, Sam Harris?"

"Things, Joseph, things. Who knows, I might wake up in the morning and decide I want to go to church."

"That'll be the day. But if you do, send me a warning because I'm staying home where it'll be safe when the church ceiling comes down on top of your head, you old sinner."

The two of them shared a bellowing laugh. Pop had spent a good part of the last twenty years trying to get Sam to join his church. But Sam always said that he didn't need any church because he had a direct line with the Lord.

After Sam bid Helen good night and thanked her again for a delicious meal, he grabbed hold of my hand, gave me a firm handshake, and said, "Now you behave yourself, young fellow, and don't give Pop here any cause to worry."

"I won't, Uncle Sam," I replied.

"I know you won't. I'll see you next weekend." All the while, I could feel Helen still imitating Sam. It always took all the strength I could muster to keep from laughing.

When Sam was finished with his goodbyes, the two friends made their way down the steps, continuing with their ritualistic conversation.

"You enjoy the day tomorrow, Joseph, and say a prayer for me just in case I can't catch up with the Lord myself. He's awful busy on Sundays."

"Hush your pagan mouth. Get home safely. I'll see you sometime on Monday."

Sam lived just two blocks away. Pop would usually walk with him to the corner of Seventh Avenue. Once Helen and I were sure they were several houses away, we turned toward each other and laughed our heads off for a good few minutes. "Have you ever seen such a pair in your life?" she asked between chuckles.

"No Ma'am," I whimsically responded.

"Well, it's late and you have to get up early for church young man, so carry yourself on inside and get ready for bed."

"Yes Ma'am." I grabbed her rocker and carried it back inside. Helen followed me to the foyer, gave me a hug, then instructed me to go get washed up and hurry to bed.

A few minutes later, I was in bed and Pop came in to wish me a good night. He pulled the sheet up over my shoulders, kissed my forehead, and said, "I love you, Son."

"I love you, too, Grandpop," I replied from the bottom of my heart. I did indeed love him. As far as I was concerned, he was the kindest person in the world.

Pop was nearly out the door when I stopped him with a question. "Did you ever find out what happened to all the food, and what the Englishman was up to?"

"I sure did, but that's another story. If you behave yourself all week, I'll tell you next Saturday."

He exited the room, closing the door behind him. A short while later, I was fast asleep dreaming about hidden treasures in darkened attics.

# CHAPTER THREE

**T**he days couldn't pass quickly enough for me. Pop had aroused my curiosity and left me hanging. Several times during the week, I tried to get him to tell me what happened to the extra food that had been prepared and what the Englishman had been up to. "Come on, Pop. Please tell me, I can't wait until Saturday," I pleaded.

"Patience, Son, patience," was his constant and only reply. So it went, until finally, after what seemed like an eternity, Saturday rolled around.

The sun had barely made its appearance in the early morning sky when I climbed out of bed. Slowly, I made my way over to the window and opened the shutters at the top and bottom, letting in the early morning light. Although it was only slightly past sunrise, I could tell it was to be another one of those hot, sticky days that were common in New York City during August.

The street below my second floor bedroom window was deserted, except for the familiar sights and sounds of the milkman as he made his deliveries. His wagon and horse were parked in front of our house, as usual. It was convenient for him to leave it there since we were nearly in the middle of the block. Besides, Pop was an early riser and never complained about the loud, clinking noises made by the empty bottles when the milkman swung the full crates onto the wagon. He would work his way down the block to Seventh Avenue on our side of the street. He would then return to his wagon, deposit the empty bottles, grab another case of milk, and make his scheduled deliveries down the other end of the street, until he reached the corner house on Eighth Avenue. Then he returned to his wagon and repeated his routine on the other side of the street. When his deliveries were finally finished, he climbed on his wagon, yanked on the reins, and signaled his horse to move on.

My head was sticking slightly out the window and my eyes followed the wagon until it turned the corner at Eighth Avenue and disappeared. I continued to survey the block. Several dogs walked slowly down the street alongside the curb. They weren't doing anything interesting enough to keep my attention, so I pulled my head back inside the window.

It didn't take me long to get dressed. As soon as I finished, I made my bed and straightened up my room. Keeping my room relatively neat was my only real responsibility around the house. I made a final visual check of my bedroom, decided everything was in order and headed downstairs where I joined Pop in the kitchen. He was sitting at the steel kitchen table reading his favorite paper, The New York Age, and sipping on a cup of coffee. When he saw me, he folded the paper in half, dropped it on the table, and greeted me. "Good morning, Goldie."

"Morning Pop," I responded cheerfully. "It's Saturday," I informed him, just in case he wasn't aware that it was. He just smiled and said, "Come on over here and give Pop a hug."

Without hesitation, I obliged him, then opened my mouth to speak. But before I could say anything, Pop placed his finger over my lips. "Now, don't you start the day off asking me about the Englishman and all the food again. This evening will be here soon enough." It was almost as if he had read my mind, because that's exactly what I was getting ready to ask him. We exchanged smiles. Pop stood up and motioned for me to have a seat. "What would you like for breakfast this morning?" he inquired.

"Eggs and bacon," was my response. I looked forward to our breakfasts together on Saturday mornings. Helen slept late and usually made her way to the kitchen just as we were finishing, complaining about the mess we had made of her kitchen.

Just as we had expected, as soon as I had bitten into my last piece of crunchy bacon, Helen made her appearance and immediately began fussing. She had good reason to complain because Pop had burned the bacon almost to a crisp, just the way he and I liked it.. He used a separate pan for the eggs and, as he did more often than not, had let the grease overheat before he put in the eggs. When Helen entered, it looked more like a disaster area than a kitchen. The counter was a mess of egg shells, spilled grease and bread crumbs. A thin layer of smoke, from the partially burned bacon and grease, still lingered in the air. Helen rattled on about how she wasn't going to clean up the mess, while she went about doing just that.

Meanwhile, I did everything I could to keep from laughing out loud, as Pop mimicked her. I was almost caught laughing once, when she turned around, but was saved by the jiggling of the bells atop the iceman's wagon. I dashed into the hallway where I hollered back to Pop, "I'll stop the iceman," I'm sure Helen heard me laughing as I dashed down the hall through the foyer and out of the door. Once down the steps, I ran and jumped over the fence just as the iceman, Mr. Watson, was returning to his wagon from making a delivery next door.

"Hi, young fellow. How are you today?" he inquired politely.

"I'm just fine, Mr. Watson, and you?"

"Just dandy. Just dandy. Would you like to feed Ginny a few carrots?" he inquired, knowing fully well that was one of the reasons I ran out to greet him. He reached under the buckboard, pulled out a handful of fresh carrots and handed them to me. Ginny was a big, strong looking, black horse with white hoofs. Mr. Watson claimed he had ridden Ginny all the way from Mississippi to New York when he first came to town, years back. Pop said no one could say if that was or wasn't true, because as far back as he could remember, Ginny had always been at the front of Mr. Watson's wagon, faithfully doing her job. While I stood stroking and feeding Ginny, Mr. Watson carted a large chunk of ice up the steps. Pop greeted him at the top of the stoop.

I watched as the two of them disappeared into the. house.

A few minutes later, they reemerged laughing and pointing at me. I didn't wonder long about what they were laughing at. A sudden and unexpected foul smell caught my nose. I had gone to Ginny's rear to play with her tail and as luck would have it, she needed to relieve herself at that very moment. So I found my shoes covered with horse droppings. I didn't find it too amusing, but Pop and Mr. Watson were rolling with laughter. I quickly looked up and down the block, hoping that no one else had seen my misfortune, then ran into the yard to clean off my shoes.

I spent a good part of the rest of the morning running in and out of the living room to check the time on the large grandfather clock next to the fireplace. Each time, hoping it was five o'clock.

It was late in the afternoon when I headed down the block to my friend Herby's house to pass away several hours, shooting marbles. We had just completed a game, and I was busy counting my winnings when I glanced up the block. Much to my delight, I saw Uncle Sam coming down the street.

Just like the accuracy of the hands of the grandfather clock in our living room, I could depend on Uncle Sam to arrive at five. His six-foot-two lean frame was easily recognized. He stood erect with his head held high and each step he took was a long strutting stride.

I didn't bother to finish counting my marbles, just dropped them into their pouch, pulled the drawstring taut, then bid my playmate a hasty farewell, as I jumped over his fence and ran to meet Uncle Sam.

When he saw me running toward him, he started jogging. He beat me to the gate by several steps, swung it open, and stepped aside, allowing me to enter the front yard first. I dashed through. Sam followed me inside, where we shook hands. As usual, he handed me the ever-present box of pastry, and together, we climbed the front steps.

Sam followed me into the kitchen, where he and Helen exchanged friendly greetings. We didn't see Pop on our way through the living room to the kitchen.

"Where's Pop?" I asked.

"He hasn't gotten back from his meeting yet," Helen replied.

"Where that man finds the time to serve on so many committees, beats me. It's bad enough that he's gone to one meeting or another just about every other evening, now he's taking to Saturday meetings, too. I keep telling him that he isn't getting any younger, and he'd better learn to take it easy on the weekends," Sam quipped.

"Oh, it wasn't a scheduled meeting or anything like that. He said that the Harlem Vocational Guidance Council was holding a special meeting," Helen informed Sam. "He should be home any minute now. Can I get you something while you're waiting?"

"A cup of coffee and a piece of what's in that box will be just fine."

I had been so excited about Sam's arrival that I hadn't opened the box of goodies he had handed me a few minutes earlier. After all, shortly after Pop arrived and we finished supper, he was going to continue his story as promised. The thought of hearing the rest had occupied most of the space in my mind for the better part of the past week.

"Pastry before supper, Sam, shame on you. I suppose you'll be wanting a piece of whatever is in the box, too, young man?" Helen stated flatly.

"Yes Mam," I answered quickly, as I opened the box. Oh, boy, doughnuts!" I shouted, turning toward Sam. "Thanks, Uncle Sam."

"Don't mention it, champ," he replied and gave me a wink. I returned it before turning my attention to the monumental task at hand; selecting a doughnut.

No more than twenty minutes had passed when I heard the front door slam shut. Pop was home. I ran to greet him.

"Well, to what do I owe this enthusiastic greeting?"

"I'm just glad you're home, Pop."

"You don't' fool old Pop. Come on, tell the truth. You're just waiting until we finish supper and I tell you what the Englishman had been up to, now aren't you?"

"That, too," I confessed. Pop rested his arm on my shoulder and we headed toward the kitchen. Just as we reached the entrance to the kitchen, he spoke. "Has that old buzzard of an uncle of yours arrived yet?" From inside the kitchen, Sam replied, "I've arrived and been sitting here starving, waiting for you to drag your slow-moving self back home." Uncle Sam stood. Pop deliberately took short, choppy steps, slowly making his way over to the table. Once there, he hunched over while slowly extending his hand for Uncle Sam to shake it. Helen and I shared a laugh as Pop and his dear friend clowned.

Pop, Uncle Sam, and I exited the kitchen and spent the next half hour seated in the living room. I flipped through a Sears catalog while the two of them engaged in a variety of conversations. Although I wasn't intentionally trying to, I couldn't help but overhear them as they chatted. Pop expressed a concern about the number of southern Negroes coming North. "It seems that the Negro population is doubling annually in New York," he noted.

"Yeah, it seems that way. It's too bad in a way. There isn't much back home for them, and unfortunately, a lot of our southern brothers and sisters will find there isn't much here for them, either."

"You said a mouthful when you said that. You're absolutely right, Sam. Let's not even mention anything pertaining to how upset certain white folks are getting about the migration."

"Certain white folks indeed, Joseph. It seems, on the surface anyway, that the white folks getting the most upset are the immigrants just arriving here from Europe."

Just the other day, when I was down at the courthouse, I overheard a couple of immigrants talking about how all the 'niggers' were stealing their jobs. Judging by their accent, I guessed that they were from Ireland. They had to be speaking for my benefit because they could barely speak English, yet they struggled with each word just so I could hear them." As I listened to them blabbing on, I thought that it was ironic that Europeans brought us over here as slaves to work for them, and now Europeans are complaining about us taking jobs. "Where does it end, Joseph, Where does it end?" Sam inquired of Pop.

"I can't answer that, Sam, but there's trouble brewing in town. Sooner or later, it's going to spill over into the streets. Just the other night some Irish boys beat up on two black boys who were trying to take a short-cut home through Canary Island."

"Must of been a couple of young fools just arrived from Mississippi or somewhere."

"You're right about that, Sam." Odds were that Sam was indeed right because anyone who was colored and had been in town longer than a month, knew that you stayed away from the area between One-hundred-thirty-eighth and One hundred forty-eighth Streets, west of Eighth Avenue, at night. If you felt pressed to venture into the area during the day, you did so at your own risk. The area was mostly unfilled marsh, and a group of white boys known as the Canary Island Gang didn't take too kindly to seeing any "darkies" or "niggers" in the area.

"I agree with you one hundred percent when you say it's going to spill over into the street. Some of our younger brothers making their way into the city ain't going to stand for it much longer."

"The way things have been going lately, it wouldn't surprise me if folks started rioting again, soon."

"Wouldn't surprise me none either, Sam. Remember the riots back in the summer of 1900?"

"I sure do. How could I forget them? How could either of us forget that? Hell, as I remember it, we both barely escaped that first night of rioting with our lives. Your grandfather and I had to spend the night in the basement of The Marshall, over on West Fifty-third Street."

"There were riots back in 1900?" I inquired. "I never heard anything about riots the year I was born."

"That's because white folks like to bury some of the things they've done to black folks. They have a convenient way of forgetting what they want to forget and remembering what they want to remember. You see, when white folks want to remember something, they write it down as they want it to be told, then they include it as fact in them history books that they use in school. When they don't want to remember something, if they write it down at all, you best believe that you'll have to go out of your way to find out where they wrote it down. The riots back in 1900 is one of those things that white folks would prefer to pretend never happened."

"You said a mouthful there, Sam Harris."

"What about the riots? How did they start? What happened?" were just a few of the questions I fired at Pop and Sam, in rapid succession.

Pop responded first, "Whoa, slow down there, son. A person ought to only ask but one question at a time, if he expects the person answering the question to do it justice. Now, let's see. I'll answer one question, and while I'm doing that, your Uncle Sam there, can dig back into his memory and see if he can find the answer to the next question. How does that sound to you, Sam?"

"Sounds just fine to me, Joseph, just fine."

The only thing that topped Pop's stories were the ones he and Uncle Sam told together. As with their cigar smoking, each tried to outdo the other when relating his part.

"Let's see," Pop began. "It was back in the summer of 1900. Believe me when I tell you that it was one of the hottest summers I can remember. Temperature must have been over ninety degrees damn near every day since the first of the month. At that time, most all of the Negroes lived down in the Forties. The area was called the Tenderloin, back then. Some folks still like to call it that. Although the actual rioting didn't begin until the 16th of August, the event that sparked them occurred during the early morning hours of the 13th. It was so hot all day on the 12th that temperatures indoors were simply unbearable. So naturally, everyone was outside sitting on their stoops, complaining about the heat and trying to get a little relief from it. That's important to know because when the actual event leading to the riots occurred, there were lots of colored folks who saw what happened. Of course, that didn't make no difference during the investigation that followed. Sam can do a better job telling you the rest of the story because he was a part of the Citizens' Protective League."

"Who were they?" I asked.

"The Citizens' Protective League was a sort of defense committee made up of prominent members of the Negro community, who conducted their own investigation into the events that triggered the actual outbreak of violence. They wanted justice," was Pop's answer as he motioned with his hand for Sam to pick up where he left off. Sam cleared his throat, leaned back in the chair, cupped his chin in his hand and began to speak.

"As near as we could determine, based on our investigation, it was somewhere late in the evening of the 12th. A young colored fellow, name of Arthur J. Harris, no kin to me, left his house over on West Forty-first Street, where he lived with his woman, to purchase a few cigars and kill a little time at the local hangout, McBride's Saloon. Around two a.m., May, Arthur's woman, came down to McBride's looking for him. After asking him to come on home, she went outside to wait for him. May was standing on the corner of Eighth Avenue and Forty-first Street waiting for Arthur, when a plain-clothes policeman, named Robert J. Thorpe, approached her and placed her under arrest for soliciting.

"Now, just as Thorpe was grabbing May to take her in custody, Arthur came out of the saloon. Arthur Harris testified at his trial that when he saw Officer Thorpe grabbing May, he had no idea at the time that he was a policeman. To him, it appeared that some white man was messing with his woman, so he did what any self-respecting man would do. He ran to her aid and began to struggle with Thorpe.

"According to Harris and several of the colored witnesses who were mulling around, Thorpe made no attempt to identify himself as a police officer. Harris claimed that he was clubbed and called a "Black son-of-a-bitch," by Thorpe, as he continued to lay his club on him. At that point, Harris, fearing for his life, pulled out a knife and cut into Thorpe. Thorpe dropped to the ground, bleeding profusely.

"Harris, fearing he had killed Thorpe, fled town and May returned to their apartment. He took a train to his mother's house, down in Washington. Although Harris felt that he had stabbed Thorpe purely in self defense, Thorpe was a white man, and if you were colored, you just didn't stab a white man to death, no matter what the reason. If they caught you and if you made it to court, more likely than not, a guilty verdict was in before the trial ever got going good. Thorpe was taken to Roosevelt Hospital, where he died the next day. May was arrested that same day at the apartment on Forty-first Street. As could be imagined, things began to heat up in town. Well, anyway, the most direct cause of the rioting was a fight between a colored man, named Spencer Walters and a white man named Thomas J. Healy, on the evening of the 15th."

"Mighty strange that Harris, Thorpe and Healy all had middle names starting with J. Don't you think so Sam?" Pop interjected.

"Hush up Joseph and let me finish the story. As the story went, the fight broke out near Thorpe's home the evening before his funeral.

"According to some witnesses we questioned, Walters was attacked by some hysterical white folks, who had just come from paying their last respects to the Thorpe family. We were never able to determine what really happened. Didn't rightly matter, because by then, any excuse for white folks to vent their anger and seek revenge for Thorpe's death would have done.

"Before anyone knew it, white folks just went plumb crazy. They seemed to show up from everywhere and nowhere, then started attacking every Negro they could find, wherever they could find them. The white mob ran up and down the streets, in and out of saloons, hotels and stores, viciously beating on virtually every colored person that they came upon. Some white street gangs took to stopping all the electric cars passing along Eighth Avenue. They dragged off every Negro aboard the cars and beat them almost senseless, on the spot.

"The police made no attempt to intervene. In fact, they participated in several of the beatings. Reserve police forces were dispatched to the area to put a stop to the beatings, but when the mostly Irish policemen arrived, they did very little to simmer things down. Some of them just stood around while others openly encouraged the rioters. The attacks went on for hours.

"The only reason the violence ended when it finally did was because a torrential thunderstorm came pouring down on the city in the early hours of the morning of the 16th.

"Both Negro and white leaders demanded that those guilty of attacking the hundreds of Negroes who were injured that night, be brought to justice. In the end, though, not much was done. The only one who was brought to 'justice' was Arthur Harris. He was arrested in Washington and extradited to New York, where he stood trial for murdering Thorpe. As was to be expected, he was found guilty of murder in the second degree and sentenced to life in prison, at hard labor. He died in Sing Sing in 1908 while folks were still fighting for his release. Yes sir, that was some summer back in 1900," Sam concluded.

I sat listening, trying to make sense of what they were saying, when Helen entered the room. "Supper's ready," she announced, almost whispering. The three of us sprung up and headed for the kitchen. Helen stood in the doorway, arms crossed, blocking the entrance. "No one sits down to a table I've prepared, without first washing their hands."

"Yes, Ma'am," we replied simultaneously.

After we had washed our hands in the bathroom down the hall, we returned to the kitchen and sat down for supper. You could tell what kind of a mood Helen had been in on a given day by what she prepared. Although she always cooked delicious meals, when Helen had what she called a "stress free day," she would make all of our favorite foods. This evening was one of those times. Supper consisted of candied yams, collard greens, black-eyed peas and best of all, an ample supply of mouth-watering corn bread.

Pop, Sam, and I stuffed ourselves. All through supper, I couldn't figure out why Helen kept smiling. When we were through eating, Sam commented first. "You out did yourself once again, Helen. Everything was delicious." He pointed a finger at Pop, who was busy wiping his mouth with his napkin, and continued. "If you ever get tired of working for this old coot, I'll double whatever he's paying you if you'll come and cook for me." Helen merely continued smiling and thanked him for the compliment. I had just finished swallowing my last mouthful of butter-drenched corn bread when Pop leaned back in his chair and began rubbing his stomach. "I'm stuffed. I couldn't fit another crumb in here," he boasted, as he patted his plump rounded belly. "Delicious, just delicious," he added.

"I'm stuffed, too," Sam commented.

"What about you, young man, have you had enough?"

"Yes Ma'am. I'm full as can be. Everything was great." I mimicked Pop as I leaned back, rubbed my stomach, and added, "I can't fit another crumb in here, either." Pop and Sam laughed at my clowning.

"Well that's too bad on all three of you because I guess you're too full to have a piece of my potato pie," Helen said teasingly, then stood to clear the dishes off the table. Pop was the first to respond. "I'm not that full. If I loosen my belt a notch or two, I suspect that I can make room for some of your pie."

"Seeing how you went to so much trouble to bake one of your famous pies, the least I can do is eat a piece," Sam chimed in. All I could do was slump in my chair and regret having stuffed myself so. There was no way I could eat anything else.

Five minutes later, Pop and Sam were digging into Helen's succulent sweet potato pie. When they had eaten their fill, Pop was the first to suggest that they retreat to the stoop and enjoy a good smoke. "You did stop off and pick up a couple of cigars, didn't you?"

"Now have I ever forgotten to bring them?"

They excused themselves from the table and headed out the kitchen. "Well you know what happens when you start getting old," Pop continued. "The old memory ain't what it used to be, you know. I'm just checking."

"Old? Are you insinuating I'm getting old, you feeble old coot?" Sam jokingly responded. They continued playfullly teasing each other on their way out of the house. Helen stood shaking her head at the two of them until they were out of hearing range. I offered to help with the dishes, not so much because I felt like performing a good deed, but I knew that the quicker the kitchen was cleaned, the sooner we could join Pop and Sam on the stoop, where Pop would continue with his story. Although he never let on, I could tell he was just as anxious to continue with his narration, as we were to hear it.

Helen and I worked at an almost feverish pace and were done cleaning the kitchen in less than twenty minutes. On the way out of the house to join Pop and Sam on the stoop, I grabbed her rocker and carried it outside.

When we appeared in the doorway, the two long-time friends, who were bent over and laughing their heads off, suddenly stopped. They sat erect and desperately tried to regain their composure. Pop managed to keep a straight face until Sam gave in and began laughing again. Pop joined him and the two of them laughed uncontrollably until Helen interrupted. "What's so funny?" she inquired.

"Oh, nothing. Nothing at all," Pop spurted out between laughs.

"Nothing, my foot. I know you, Joseph Cinque Covington, and I know you, Sam Harris. Who you two been talking about now?"

"Well, if you must know, we were talking about Pig Foot Mary," Sam volunteered.

"What un-Christian things were you saying about her?"

"Now don't go jumping to conclusions. We weren't saying anything that isn't true." Pop's reply caused Sam to start laughing again and Pop couldn't help but join him.

"I could use a good laugh myself, so long as you ain't saying nothing unkind about her," Helen stated.

"Who is Pig Foot Mary?" I inquired.

"Lillian Harris," Pop answered. He and Sam wound down their laughter.

"Big Amazon of a woman. Sells pigs' feet out of a steaming boiler mounted on a baby carriage," Sam added. "You mean to tell me you haven't seen her in front of Rudolph's saloon on Sixty-first and Amsterdam, when we pass there?"

"No, Sir," I answered in a clear tone.

"You must be half blind, Son," Pop chimed in. The two of them began to laugh again.

"Must have a problem with his nose, too. Lord knows if you can't see her big as she is, you can't miss the smell of those pig feets steaming," Sam contributed to Pop's slight teasing. Whenever the two of them were teasing each other, or someone else, they changed their normal speech patterns.

"You two can laugh at her all you want. Rumor has it that she only had five dollars to her name, when she arrived in town a couple of years ago. Now people come from miles around to get their share of her pigs' feet.

"She's making lots of money selling them pigs' feet, and ain't nothing funny about that," Helen said with a stern look on her face.

Helen was about to continue speaking, when Sam cut her off. "Actually, we weren't laughing at her."

"Well what were you laughing at?"

"Now let me see," Sam replied as he leaned back and began scratching his head. "Oh yeah, I remember now." He fought to keep a straight face while Pop was still beside himself with laughter. "Joseph over there was trying to tell me that he didn't understand how anybody could eat a pig's foot that come out of a steamer perched atop a baby carriage. Now, me, I told him that I couldn't see how nobody could eat a pig's foot, no matter where or how it was cooked. Then I asked Joseph, over there, when was the last time that he ate some pigs' feet. Well he tried to tell me that he ain't never ate no pig's foot. So I was just reminding him of a few years back, when I seen him sucking on a pig foot at a church picnic, over in Weeksville. He sucked that pig's foot clear down to the bare knuckles. Yes, he did. Seen him swallowing some chitlins, too. Yes, I did."

"Course, he claims he don't remember none of that. Now I ain't saying he liked them, 'cause I don't rightly know. I know for sure that he was a sucking on some pigs' feet that particular Sunday over in Brooklyn, because he had eyes for this church sister, name of Mabel Jenkins. She was the one who cooked them pigs' feet and chitlins, and brung them to the picnic. As much as he wanted to get to know Mabel at the time, believe me when I tell you, he would have eaten the whole pig had she cooked it and brung it with her."

"Ifin ya gonna tell the story, Sam, tell the whole story. Now I don't rightly know if Mr. Sam Harris, Attorney at Law, is speaking in truth when he sez that he ain't never ate no pig foots, but I know for sure that he's lying when he sez that he ain't never tasted no chitlins."

While Pop spoke, Sam took his turn at laughing. I joined them in their laughter. They were funny to listen to and watch. Each was trying to outdo the other, with his deliberate distortion of the English language and accompanying facial expressions. Helen was rocking in her chair, and shaking her head back and forth.

"You see, what we were really laughing about is the reason why Sam Harris gave up eating chitlins. Round about the same time I had my eye on foxy Mabel, Sam there, he had his eye on a friend of hers at the picnic, named Louise. Pretty young thing, she was. Now Sam, there didn't know that she had a eye for him, and she didn't know that Sam was eyeing her. 'Cause if they knew what each other was thinking, Sam coulda saved himself some pain, and Louise coulda saved herself some embarrassment. You see, your Uncle Sam, there, he wasn't as smooth with the ladies as I was. While he was trying to figure out how to approach Louise, I was making my move on Mabel."

"Yeah sucking on them pigs' feet and swallowing them chitlins," Sam added, when Pop paused to catch his breath.

"Say what you want, Sam Harris, but I'm gonna tell it like it was. Like I said before, while Sam was at a loss over what to do to get Louise's attention, I was making my move. All the time, Louise was hanging nearby and checking me and Mabel out. She figured that there must be some truth in that old saying that 'the way to a man's heart is through his stomach,' because I was carrying on so, about how great a cook Mabel was.

"Now mind ya, it was a task, eating them pig foots and chitlins, but a man who thinks he's in love will do anything. Even suck on a pig's foot and swallow a chitlin," Pop quickly added to his previous sentence before he paused, looked at Sam, nodded his head and continued. "Since Sam hadn't made a move, there weren't nothing left for Louise to do, except approach him. She asked Mabel and I, what she should do. I told her that Sam loved him some home cooked pig foots and chitlins, and that she should invite him over for a nice home cooked pot of them. She took my advice and invited him over to her place on the following Sunday, for supper. Mind you, she didn't tell him what she was fixing."

"Mabel and Louise lived in the same building, so when Sunday rolled around, I made it a point to be at Mabel's place, 'cause I knew something that Sam didn't. Louise wasn't no cook. I had let Sam know that I was gonna be at Mabel's, and that he and Louise should drop on down after supper."

"It must have been near seven in the evening, when I arrived at the building. I was halfway up the steps when the nastiest smell that I ever run across hit me smack in the face and damned near knocked me back down the steps. 'Jesus Christ!' I shouted. 'Smell like a thousand skunks done crawled in the building and died.' I pulled out my handkerchief, covered my nose, and fought my way through the sickening smell back up the steps. On the way up, I noticed that everyone in the building had their windows opened. Half of the residents were leaning out of their windows, mumbling to themselves, and sucking in air.

"Just as I was about to open the door to the building, Mabel swung it open and came out shaking her head and holding her nose. I wasted no time in asking her what the hell was that funk. It turned out that Louise had cooked a whole ten-pound pot of chitlins, pig foots mixed right in, without bothering to clean the chitlins. Sam, there, not wanting to hurt her feelings went on and ate some of them uncleaned, overcooked, foul smelling chitlins. Need I tell you what them pigs' intestines did to his intestines? The man spent the next two weeks a sitting on a toilet stool." Pop burst out laughing.

"All right, enough about pig feet and chitterlings, Joseph Cinque. You've had Goldie and I sitting on pins and needles all week waiting for you to finish up where you left off last week," Helen interjected.

"Yeah Pop, I've been waiting all week for tonight to come."

"Okay, relax, you two. Just give me a chance to get myself together here," Pop said, as he let out a deep breath. Meanwhile, Sam had been laughing so hard he was in tears. He pulled out his handkerchief and wiped his face. It took them a couple of minutes to simmer down. Once they had, Pop took his story-telling position, and Sam got comfortable in his. At long last, I thought. I'm finally going to find out what happened to all that food, and what the Englishman had been up to back in the 1850s.

# CHAPTER FOUR

After his usual opening statement, Pop devoted the next fifteen minutes to summing up his story from the previous Saturday. What he really was doing, was attempting to keep me in suspense as long as he could. I say me and not us because I suspected that Sam and Helen had been blessed previously with Pop's oral recount of history.

"Now, let's see. Oh yeah, as I was telling you last week. When I was fourteen, I became aware that there was something strange going on around the farm at least one weekend each month. It had been close to four years since I discovered my mother's belongings tucked away in the steamer trunk in the attic. Whatever it was that led her to save all those clippings in her scrapbooks had placed its compelling hold on me. Adding to the collection that my mother began was more than a pastime with me. It had become an obsession."

"For the past few years, my thirst for further information concerning the articles in my mother's scrapbooks seemed insatiable. I religiously clipped and saved all the related newspaper clippings I could get my hands on. I also began asking a lot of questions of George and the other servants. George usually left my questions unanswered. He would only respond to my constant barrage by telling me, 'You're too young to understand what's going on. When Mr. Covington thinks you're old enough to understand, he'll answer your questions."

"You mean my father," I blurted out in anger.

'Trust me, Joseph, Mr. Covington will answer all your questions in due time. Don't approach him. You know as well as I do that he has his ways about him. He'll approach you in good time,' George continued, as if he hadn't heard my reference to his insistence on never referring to the Englishman as my father. I had come to grow weary of the game that everyone seemed to play when it came to the relationship that existed between the Englishman and myself. Hell, it wasn't any secret that Mr. John Covington, as everyone else called the Englishman, was my father; he helped to conceive me.

"George was loyal to the Englishman almost to a fault. After a while, I started questioning him about the Englishman more out of a desire to annoy him than to extract answers from him. At best, on rare occasions, usually when he had taken one swig too many from his jug of corn whiskey, George would slip and let little tidbits of information escape from his lips. When he was in his spirits, I could hit him with two or three questions, to which he would respond before he realized that he was talking too much for his own good. Once he became aware that I was attempting to take advantage of the loosened condition of his lips brought on by his consumption of too much liquor, he would clam-up.

"The way he did it was always amusing to me. He would press his index finger against his lips and repeat aloud to himself, 'Shush George Black, shush George Black,' then he would shout at me to go away and leave him alone. I never managed to extract any information from him that in and of itself answered any of the questions I put to him in his inebriated condition.

"Subconsciously, he must have been aware that he was about to give up some information that he shouldn't be divulging because the few words he blurted out amounted to no more than jibberish or riddles. His fragmented and incomplete responses to my questions just supplied me with additional pieces of the puzzle to fit in place.

"Early in the beginning of my attempts to extract answers, I found out that if I pretended to know about something, other people would gladly volunteer additional information. Armed with that discovery, I would take a phrase or a key word which George let slip, approach one of the workers or servants, and begin a conversation while making use of what little information George involuntarily divulged. Most of them didn't know much, so I narrowed it down to two others, who might hold the missing pieces to the puzzle.

"In addition to George, there were two other Negro workers on the farm who had been around since the Englishman purchased it back in thirty-nine. Their names were Chester and Ben.

"Chester was in charge of the farm workers. I never felt easy around him. When I was younger, there was something about him that scared me. Perhaps it was the fact that he was such a large man. He stood a good six feet, seven inches tall and weighed at least three hundred pounds. His blemish-free complexion was nearly jet black and his features were distinctively African. George once told me that Chester was a descendant of African royalty. Whether that was true or not, I had no way of telling. There was, however, an air about him that seemed to back up George's story. He strutted instead of walking in a more natural manner. His head was always held high. The other workers looked up to him and seemed to almost pay him homage. Now that I was in my teens, I wasn't scared of him anymore, but he still seemed a bit strange.

"When Chester wasn't tending the land, he kept to himself. He had a two-room cabin a few feet away from the barn. The only people that I ever saw him warm up to were George and Ben. Ben was in charge of all the animals. When Chester wasn't issuing instructions to the workers, his jaws were locked shut. Outside of seeing him conversing with George and Ben, the only other person I ever saw him talking with was the Englishman. The two of them would stay huddled up inside his cabin for hours conversing, mostly in hushed tones. I knew that it would be pointless to try and extract any information from him. Ben was my best bet for filling in the blanks.

"Unlike Chester, Ben loved to run his mouth. Of course, like everyone else around the place, he seemed to act as if the manner in which the Englishman came and went was nothing worth raising an eyebrow over. Like George, he enjoyed sipping from a jug full of corn whiskey. Unlike George, he spoke in complete sentences. The only problem was that each succeeding sentence was unrelated to the previous one. However, it was through Ben's rumblings that I got the bits of information which gave me the final hints of what was probably behind the Englishman's strange arrivals and the disappearance of all the food prepared the day after he returned home.

"One Saturday night, when the Englishman was still away, after everyone else had gone to sleep, I quietly slipped out of the house and made my way to Ben's cabin, which was about a quarter of a mile down from the main house. I figured he would be a bit out of it by then. Just after sunset, on Saturdays, he would start sipping from his jug and by the time everyone else had gone to bed for the evening, he would be skunk drunk.

"There was a full moon that particular evening and its rays illuminated the path to Ben's cabin. Halfway down, I stopped dead in my tracks. A thought struck me. I slapped myself upside the head. Ben was in charge of the farm animals, yet he lived in the cabin closest to the fields. On the other hand, Chester, who was in charge of the fields, lived in the cabin next to the barns and stockyards. That's odd, I thought. For several moments, I stood looking up at the brightly lit moon and rubbing my hand down my cheeks, which is something that I did whenever I was puzzled. At first, I was a little angry with myself for not noticing that oddity before. That, coupled with the seemingly secret meetings between the Englishman and Chester, with George occasionally in attendance, led me to suspect that whatever the Englishman was up to, involved the barn. I stood there for a moment longer trying to decide if I should continue on to Ben's cabin, or if I could learn more by snooping around the barn.

"My first decision was to head toward the barn but, as I turned back toward the house, I remembered that it was always locked securely at night. For the first time, I thought that, too, was strange. How could I have been so blind as not to see all of the clues that had been staring me practically in the face. Unless there was something in the barn that no one was supposed to see, why was it kept locked? I slapped myself on the forehead again once I realized that for the past couple of years, I had observed Chester unlocking the barn doors in the morning when Ben arrived to let out the animals. Once they were herded out, he locked it back. He re-opened the barn in the late evening and after Ben put the animals in for the night, Chester locked the doors again. The only time that the barn was unlocked in the day was when Ben was cleaning the stables. When he was done, he would stay close to the barn until Chester returned to lock it. In fact, no one ever entered the barn, unless they were accompanied by Chester or Ben, yet I paid it no mind.

"There's no point in heading back to snoop around the barn, I thought. It's locked tight. Perhaps Ben will let something slip, I concluded and decided to continue on my way. If I can get inside the barn, I'll probably find answers to many of my questions. If I could figure out how to get inside, when would be the safest time to do it? I'm a goner for sure if Chester catches me in there. I shuddered at visions of Chester sneaking up behind me while I was snooping around in the barn, yanking me clear off my feet and shaking a good dozen or so years off the tail end of my life.

"Although I often had an over-active imagination, I knew that I would take the risk of being caught by him because I had become obsessed with finding out what was going on about the farm. It may take me a while, but I'll find a way into the barn, and then I'll be able to find out what deep dark secrets lay hidden inside, was my last thought, before I arrived at the entrance to Ben's cabin.

"I took extreme care not to make any noise as I crept up to the door and pressed my ear against it. Inside, I could hear Ben mumbling to himself. He was rambling on about a hidden railroad and how they were going to sell him into slavery down South if they found it. 'Railroad?' There's no railroad anywhere near here. Wait a minute! No! He couldn't be talking about that railroad,' I asked myself aloud.

"In an attempt to hear better what he was saying, I leaned closer to the door. My weight pressing against it caused it to swing open. I tumbled forward and landed on the floor, just inside the cabin.

"My sudden and unexpected entrance took its toll on Ben. I never saw a person jump as far as he did. He sprang to his feet damn near busting his head on the cabin's low ceiling. Normally, his sudden movement, combined with the unplanned manner in which I entered his cabin, would have given me quite a jolt myself, but the look on Ben's face caused me to forget all about my condition. He looked as if I were the devil himself come to call on him. His face turned white momentarily, and considering his ebony complexion, that was a sight to behold in and of itself. Immediately, I stood up and began to wipe the dust off my shirt and trousers.

"It took Ben a full minute before he was able to regain his composure once he realized that it was only me. 'Ya just took twenty years off the tail end of my life. I ought to skin ya good boy! What ya doin' sneakin' round here at night? How come ya ain't up at the house like ya ought to be? Didn't any of dem fancy teachers of yours teach ya to knock fore ya come a bustin' into a body's home? I asked ya what ya doing snoopin' round my place boy?' Ben shouted.

I opened my mouth to answer, but he cut me off. Where's my jug. If ever I needed a sip, I needs one now. Lord, chile, what ya done ain't nice. Ya trying to give old Ben a heart attack, is ya?'

"He wasn't shouting any longer, and that was a relief. Ben uncorked his jug, tilted his head back and took a long swig.

"I took advantage of his lips being temporarily occupied to try and offer him an acceptable explanation as to why I had suddenly come tumbling into his cabin. "I was down by the stream, and I decided to take the long way home. I was passing by when I thought I heard a loud noise inside your cabin. I was on my way to see if everything was all right when I tripped on a loose board on the porch and fell against the door,' I blurted nervously. All the while I spoke, I kept my fingers crossed behind my back, hoping Ben would accept my flimsy explanation.

"Ben lowered the jug, wiped his mouth on his shirt sleeve and stared at me. We stood looking dead into each other's eyes, me trying to see if he believed my story and him trying to see if I was telling the truth.

"Ben broke the silence. 'What loose board? There ain't no loose board out there.'

"My heart dropped to my stomach. He doesn't believe me. What other lie can I tell, I worried to myself. Fortunately, before I tried to offer him another explanation he started laughing.

" 'Ya probably tripped over your own feets. Ya been a tripping over things since ya wuz no higher than my kneecaps. Close the door and come on in youngin. It's been years since ya paid old Ben a visit. Ya use to visit me all the time when I lived up the hill.' Up the hill was how he referred to the cabin that Chester now occupied. When he made reference to up the hill, bells went off in my head.

"That's right, I thought. It was only a few years ago that Chester and Ben traded cabins. Shortly after that, Chester began locking the barn, the Englishman arrived home in the middle of the night, and the cook prepared seemingly excessive amounts of food upon his arrival.

"My thoughts were interrupted by the sound of Ben's groveled voice. 'So how is ya getting along lately?'

"Fine, Sir, just fine.'"

"You oughtn't be calling me Sir. Was a time when ya use to call me Uncle Ben. Cause ya was just a little tyke then. Now look at ya, damn near all growed up. Does my heart good to see ya standing dere so tall. Course you need to put a little weight on dem bones of yerns. If ya grows any longer, the next time ya visit old Ben ya won't be able to stand as straight in here as ya is now. Have a seat and stay a spell.'

"Yes Sir. I mean, Uncle Ben."

"Ya too growed up to be calling me Sir or Uncle Ben. Grown fellow like you can call me Ben, same as everyone else 'round here does.' Ben paused long enough to take another swig from his jug. 'Ain't got nothing to offer ya, except what's in this jug and ya ain't old enough for dat yet. Ya want some water. I got plenty of dat.'

"That's okay. I'm not thirsty. Why don't you take a swig for me," I encouraged, hedging him on to getting drunk to the point where he would become an easy mark for a few of my many questions.

Silence hung over the room as he returned the jug to his lips and tilted his head back. This time he took three long gulps of liquor before he brought his head forward and separated his lips from the jug.

" 'Ah,' he blurted out as he shook his head and wiped his lips on his shirt sleeve, which was something that he seemed to do more out of habit than need. He valued his liquor too much to waste a drop or two by missing his mouth, so there really wasn't anything to wipe.

" 'Now let's see. Where wuz I? Oh yeah I wuz commenting on how growed up ya done got. Pretty soon fore ya know it, ya be takin off from here looking about Mr. Covington's business for him.'

"Mr. Covington! Mr. Covington! He's my father damn it, my father. Why won't anyone refer to him as my father? I shouted angrily to myself. I calmed myself and responded out loud to Ben's last remark. 'I suspect that soon I will be looking after the Englishman's business.'

"It was apparent to anyone who heard me address my father, the Revered Mr. Covington, as the Englishman that I was full of resentment and anger. It wasn't as if the Englishman himself denied being my father. Out of respect, as was the way of things back then, I had been taught to address him as 'Sir'. It just seemed that everyone else around the farm was bent on pretending that the relationship between the Englishman and me was not a blood relationship. On the few occasions I attempted to bring up the subject of how everyone seemed not to want to acknowledge the fact that I was his son, the Englishman put me off.

" 'What other people think isn't important,' he would say. 'What is important is that you and I know what we are to each other. When you are old enough to understand, there are a lot of things that I will tell you that will help explain why things are the way they are now.'

"At fourteen, I could no longer be put off with such vague statements. Whatever the 'lots of things' were, I was determined to find them out long before the Englishman decided I was old enough to know them.

" 'What ya day dreamin' bout boy?' Ben's voice startled me; I had been lost in my thoughts.

" 'Me? I ain't been day dreaming. I was thinking,' I quickly replied.

" 'Thinkin', day dreaming, all the same to a boy your age. Tell old Ben what ya waz thinkin' bout.'

"Judging by the manner in which he was slurring his words together as he spoke, I could tell that the last few swigs had taken there toll on him. If I'm going to get any information out of old Ben tonight, I'd better start now before he passes out, I surmised.

" 'Come on youngin, tell me what ya wuz thinkin', "Ben pleaded as his head wobbled forward. 'I knows that ya wuz daydreaming about somethin', cause when I looked over at ya, ya sure wuzn't in this room.'

" 'I was wondering what it was like to ride on a railroad train,' I quickly blurted out in an attempt to find out what he had been mumbling about when I crept up to his cabin a few minutes earlier.

" 'What ya talking' bout?' Ben snapped. 'There ain't no railroad no wheres near here. So where ya gonna find one to ride?' Judging by Ben's reaction to my statement I quickly surmised that I had struck a nerve.

" 'I heard a rumor in town that they were planning to build one near here.'

" 'Ya ain't heard no such thing.'

" 'Did too. Even heard you talking about it when I was getting ready to knock on your door before I tripped.'

"What did I say that for. Before I could complete my sentence good, Ben jumped to his feet and began shouting at me.

" Now ya listens to me and ya listens to me good.

Ya ain't never heard me say nothin bout no railroad. If you know what's good for ya youngin, ya won't go around asking nobody 'bout no railroad in these parts,' he raved on.

"It was obvious that I had hit the right button. Ben's almost violent reaction to my statement all but confirmed my earlier suspicion. He was somehow involved with the Underground Railroad and was afraid of getting caught. I decided to press on. I hadn't anything to lose by pushing the point. He's so drunk now that he won't remember much about what's said tonight in the morning, I rationalized to myself.

" 'I could swear that I heard you say something about taking a ride south on a railroad.'

"'Ya don't know what ya is saying'. All I knows about is takin care of the animals and I does a good job of that.' The fear in his voice was apparent. 'If ya knows what's best for ya youngin, ya better get on home and don't go botherin' me no more 'bout somethin ya thinks ya heard me say dat I didn't say.'

Ben pressed his jug of whiskey tight against his lips and took a long deliberate swallow. All the while he drank, he stared directly at me with his eyes bulging wide with fear.

"My suspicion was confirmed. The railroad that Ben was afraid of getting caught messing with was indeed the Underground Railroad. The newspapers that the Englishman brought with him from the big city often carried stories about the Underground Railroad. Occasionally, the local paper also contained an article about it. Whenever I ran across an article about the Underground Railroad, I read it carefully, tore it from the newspaper and read it several more times before I added it to my collection stowed away in the attic. The whole concept of the Underground Railroad fascinated me.

"Locked barn, disappearing food, strange comings and goings in the night, Underground Railroad, it's all starting to add up now, was what I was thinking when Ben finally lowered his jug and disrupted my thoughts.

"Before he could say anything else I spoke. 'You're right. I probably misunderstood what I thought I heard you say. Forget I said anything.'

"My words seemed to have a calming effect on Ben. He leaned back against the wall and studied me for a good two minutes before replying.

" 'Ya go on and get out of here now. Ya oughtn't not be out so late.'

" 'Yes sir, Uncle Ben. You're right. I better get home now.' I stood up and headed for the door. Ben struggled to his feet, staggered over to where I stood and draped his arm around my shoulders. 'Come visit your old uncle again real soon. Ya hear me?'

" 'Yes Sir, I mean Uncle Ben.' Ben dropped his arm from my shoulders, and while struggling to maintain his balance, made his way to the door and swung it open.

" 'Are you okay?' I asked.

" 'I'm fit as can be,' he blurted. I patted him on the back as I walked past him out into the cool night air, then turned to bid him good night just in time to see him passing out. My attempt to reach him before he collapsed was in vain. His body made a loud thumping sound as it made contact with the hard wooden floor of the cabin. I bent over, wrapped my arms securely around his waist, partially lifted him up, and dragged his limp body across the room over to the bed.

"After struggling to get him on the bed, I removed his shoes and grabbed hold of the blanket at the foot of the bed. The flickering light from the kerosene lamp on the table next to the bed bounced off his face. A strange feeling gripped me as I stood looking at Ben. For the first time in my life, I studied his every feature. His face seemed to tell a story. His wrinkled forehead, gray hair, and eyebrows seemed a testimony to a lifetime of hard work and painful memories.

"George once told me that Ben was a former slave, but no one knew how he got his freedom or in which state he had been a slave. George went on to say he suspected that Mr. Covington had purchased Ben and given him his freedom, but neither Ben nor Mr. Covington ever confirmed that. Once, shortly after I found my mother's trunk in the attic, when I attempted to question Ben about what it was like to be a slave, he angrily replied, 'Can't nobody tell what its like bein' a slave to nobody dat ain't been one.' That was all he said except to add, 'I don't wanna talk bout it because it makes me hurt too much way down inside'. After hearing Ben mumbling about the railroad earlier, I concluded that his freedom probably came via the Underground Railroad.

"I gently pulled the blanket over Ben's still body, then leaned over to blow out the lamp. Just as I was about to lift the globe from the lamp and blow out the flame, I noticed the chain around his neck. Ever since I could remember, he had worn that chain securely tucked inside his shirt. The one time I questioned him about what was at the end of it, he damned near snapped my head off.

" 'Something to keep evil spirits away is at the end of dis here chain boy, and can't nobody look upon it 'ceptin' me. Cause if dey do, it'll blind them.' It wasn't what he said, as much as it was the way he said it that scared me. I was only seven years old at the time.

"Although I discounted his story as I got older, I never asked him about the chain again. Being the overly curious person that I had become, I wasn't going to let the opportunity to satisfy one of my childhood curiosities pass. Without hesitating a second longer, I reached over and carefully placed my hand on the chain. It felt cold to my touch. A chill shot through my body and I momentarily released my grip. For a fleeting moment, I wondered if there had been any truth to what Ben had told me about what was at the end of it.

"'Get a hold of yourself. Probably ain't nothing at the end of the chain except a locket or something like that,' I said to myself in an attempt to bolster my courage. I placed my hand back on the chain and began pulling it up. It was long and I could feel the weight of whatever it was at the end.

"The possibility of Ben waking wasn't the reason that I was slowly and deliberately taking my time; the effects of the whiskey insured that he wouldn't awaken. A subtle fear still lingered in me. My imagination momentarily got the best of me. Visions of rays of light with blinding intensity shooting out from whatever was at the end of the chain and blinding me for life danced through my head. "Get a hold of yourself! I commanded myself again. You're too old to believe in such foolishness." Obedient to my command, I regained my composure and pulled the remainder of the chain out of Ben's shirt.

"All that worry for nothing was all I could think of when I saw the object of my initial fear. Wait a minute! It can't be! No, nothing's this easy, were a few of my thoughts as I reached for the object at the end of the chain and lifted it up. My eyes were fixed on the key that dangled from the chain. If these key fits where I think it fits, all my wondering will be over.

"With that thought in mind, I carefully leaned over, lifted Ben's head and slipped the chain from around his neck. He didn't stir an inch. He was out cold and I reasoned that he would remain unconscious for quite a while. Certainly, long enough for me to confirm my suspicions concerning my find and return the key. It all went well, as I hoped it would, Ben would never even know that I had borrowed the key. Without wasting another minute, I tucked the chain and key securely in my pocket and dashed out of the cabin.

"The tension mounted in me as I speedily ran down the road back toward the main house. The full moon was still shining down on the road lighting my way. The occasional hooting sounds of the owls that lurked about sent chills up and down my spine. A quarter of the way down the road, I stopped to catch my breath and reorganize my thoughts. I can feel it. This key fits the barn. What a stroke of luck. Now, if my luck holds out, I'll get in and out of the barn without anyone seeing me.

"Judging by the position of the moon in the sky, I guessed it to be close to midnight, give or take a few minutes either way. Chester should be asleep by now. Just to play it safe, I'll sneak around the back and check things out first. Everything should be okay. Satisfied with that thought, I carefully continued on.

"As an added precaution, on my way to the barn, I quietly crept up next to Chester's cabin and peeked in the window. Aided by the moonlight, I saw him sprawled across his bed. he was snoring loudly and seemed to be in a deep sleep.

"Everything was quiet and still about the place, except for the chirping of the crickets and the continued hooting of the owls. Pressing my body tightly against the side of the barn, I slowly poked my head around the front. It seemed safe enough. Still, ever so cautiously, I made my way to the barn door. I crossed the fingers of one hand, and I slowly inserted the key in the lock. Would it fit?

"My self-imposed question was soon answered. The key slid into the keyhole with the greatest of ease and I wasted no time in turning it. Once the door was unlocked, I took another look around, quickly opened the door, slipped into the barn, and pulled the door tightly shut behind me. My heart almost dropped to the ground as several of the horses began to whimper. 'Shhh, shhh, shhh,' I pleaded as I ran from horse to horse and gently patted each one. Much to my relief, they quieted down.

"Almost tip-toeing, I made my way back over to the barn door and inched it open. If Chester had been awakened by the horses whimpering, I was up the creek without a paddle. I stood behind the door of the darkened barn and fixed my eyes on Chester's cabin. Luck was still on my side. Still aiming to play it safe, I gazed out at the cabin for a good two minutes before I closed the barn door again.

"It didn't take me long to find the lantern next to the door. Next to it was a cup where matches were kept. I took a match out, struck it against the barn wall, and lit the lantern. Unknown to me, the wick was all the way up and when I lit it, the ensuing bright light and flame almost scared me witless. The fact that I didn't drop the lantern amazes me to this day.

"Once I had everything under control again, I turned the wick down, dimming the lantern, and set out to explore the barn. Somewhere inside there was a well-guarded secret. Based on my earlier conversation with Ben, I had a pretty good idea what I was looking for. If in fact, as my suspicions told me, the farm was one of the stops for the Underground Railroad, then surely the barn had to be where the 'passengers' spent a night or two before moving on. Most likely, they were ferried across the Long Island Sound to Connecticut. From there, they were most likely led to Canada and freedom.

"From my extensive reading, I knew that the Underground Railroad was a network of people who sheltered and aided escaping slaves as they made their way out of the South and the bonds of slavery to the safety of the North or Canadian borders. Living in partial isolation on the farm provided me with plenty of time to ponder the things I read about and all the events that went on. When I first began reading about slavery and grasped what it was all about, I quickly sensed that it was wrong.

"What puzzled me most about the institution of slavery was that it existed in America. My numerous tutors had taught me about the history of the settlement of America and the reasons given for the American Revolution. If what they said was accurate, how could a nation mostly made up of people who fled their own motherland in search of new liberties and who revolted against England on the grounds of 'freedom and equality for all men,' condone slavery? If I, who was merely a child, didn't believe that slaves were not people, as proponents of slavery tried to have others believe, then surely no one believed that argument, not even those who preached it. By my twelfth birthday, I had concluded that there was an inherent evil associated with slavery that would linger on long after it was abolished. I knew deep in my heart that something as evil as American slavery couldn't last much longer. I promised myself that when I was old enough, I would actively join in the fight to end it. My heroes were the men and women I read about who were referred to as abolitionists. The thought that all along the Englishman, my father, whom I had come to despise because of the manner in which he raised me, was one of my heroes left me confused.

"There will be plenty of time to try and sort out my feelings later, I thought as I made my way in and out of the stalls, looking for a trap door.

"It didn't take much reasoning to surmise that if the barn was where they were hiding the runaway slaves, there had to be a hidden room or rooms where they were sheltered overnight. The only place that they could build such a room in the barn was underground. The entrance to the room had to be accessible, yet easily hidden. The stalls seemed the most logical place to conceal an entrance. A horse could be moved in and out of a stall with ease. Once the runaway slaves were safely in their hideaway, the hay could be thrown over the entrance to conceal it and the horse put back in the stall. Horses were always shitting all over the place. More than likely, it wouldn't be long before the horse would relieve itself in the stall that housed the entrance to the hidden room, adding more camouflage.

"Finding the hidden room that I was convinced existed, was dirty, disgusting work. It required that I search each stall on my hands and knees. Being a bit nervous and anxious, I was in a rush to find what I had come looking for.

"The first stall was empty, so I didn't give any thought to looking down before I dropped to my knees to begin my search. That was a mistake because I knelt in a pile of horse droppings. I twisted my face in disgust at the squishing sound the horse shit made as it meshed between my knees. 'Great!' I murmured aloud.

"The worst was yet to come because I had to use my hands to shift through the bed of straw covering the floor. I hadn't thought to bring along something to brush aside the mess, and I certainly wasn't risking a trip to the tool shed, which was less than four feet from Chester's cabins, to get something.

"Wading and pushing aside piles of manure was but a small price to pay for a chance to solve the puzzle that I had been working on for so long. Most of the stalls had horses in them. So stall by stall, I had to first remove the horse and pray that it didn't make any noise.

"By the time I reached the sixth stall, I had become oblivious to the manure, which covered my pants and hands. The stall was empty and that was a relief because my heart almost stopped beating each time I had to pull a horse from one before I searched it. It was the same every time I returned the animal. A good whimper from one could trigger a chain reaction from the other horses and then I was a goner for sure. In my haste to get into the barn, I hadn't given any thought to how I would escape should Chester become aroused by a number of the horses neighing at once. Surely, if they made enough noise to wake him, he would head straight for the barn.

"Since I spent a lot of time during the day playing with the horses, I felt relatively secure that I was not a stranger to them and therefore could move about without alarming them. Nevertheless, there existed the possibility that one of them would not take kindly to being disturbed in the middle of the night.

"Before entering the stall, I held the lantern at arms length and took a look at myself. What a mess, was all I could say. My hands and pants were covered with manure. A few times, I thought I would throw up from the wretched stench, but managed to refrain. There were a dozen and a half stall in the barn. With my luck, I mumbled to myself; I'll probably find what I'm looking for in the last stall.

"With extreme care, just as during the previous five times, I placed the lantern on the floor of the stall in front of me, and knelt to continue my search. With a flickering motion of my hands I brushed the hay aside hoping to find a trap door. Suddenly my fingers touched something cold. I reached for the lantern and pulled it closer. 'I knew it!' I shouted aloud before I caught myself.

"I slapped my hand across my mouth, my heart pounded rapidly. That was a mistake because I had forgotten about the manure on my hands. Now it was spread across my face as well. That didn't bother me very much at the moment. It was well worth it, considering my discovery. I quickly regained my composure and turned my attention back to the object I had just felt. The light reflected off a large brass ring.

"As soon as I calmed down a bit, I brushed aside more hay. The outline of a door was clearly visible. I grabbed hold of the lantern with one hand, firmly grasped the brass ring with the other and slowly stood. Halfway up, I paused as a tingling feeling passed through my entire body. It was as if something had escaped from the side of the now partially opened trap door and passed through me. For a split second, I wanted to release my grip on the brass ring and flee the barn. I swayed, then shook off the panicky feeling that had just come over me and opened the door until it rested against the back wall of the stall. Ever so slowly and extremely carefully, I extended the lantern in front of me in order to light up the dark, forbidden entrance beyond the door.

"My heart beat at what seemed like a hundred miles an hour as I made my way down the steep flight of steps. When I reached the bottom, I surveyed my discovery. It was a large room, measuring a good thirty-five feet from one end to the other. In the middle, there was a long table surrounded by a dozen or so crude, wooden stools. The ceiling was low and my head nearly scraped the top as I moved about in the dim light. In one corner, there was a pile of blankets and in a second, several buckets. On the wall opposite the steps, I discovered a ventilation hole. It undoubtedly led to the outside somewhere, where it was cleverly concealed. I'll search for it tomorrow, was what passed through my mind as I continued to look about the room. It was immaculately clean. So, Ben was cleaning more than stables when he was holed up in here all day on the Mondays after the Englishman returned to the farm.

"I walked over to the table in the center of the room and placed the lantern on it allowing me to see the entire room.

" 'So this explains why the Englishman appeared to always be sneaking back to his own home late at night. This is where all the food was disappearing to. 'What next,' I spoke aloud.

"It wasn't clear to me what I would do at having uncovered the Englishman's well-guarded secret. 'I'll figure that out later,' I continued as part of my one-way dialog. The next thought that crossed my now overly stimulated mind was getting Ben's key back around his neck.

"I made sure that I didn't leave any tell-tale signs that anyone had been there, then exited the barn. Within seconds, I re-locked the door, then wiped the latch and lock clean with the end of my shirt. I glanced at Chester's cabin to insure myself that he hadn't been aroused, then carefully made my way to the back of the barn where I removed my shirt and used it to wipe the horse manure form my face, hands, and the front of my pants. I then plotted how to cover the rest of my tracks.

"What a mess. After I get the key back around Ben's neck, I'll go down to the stream and jump in, clothes and all. If George sees my clothes like they are now, it won't take him much thinking to figure out where I've been. If I hang them outside my window, they should be dry by morning and no one will be the wiser.'

"Getting the key back around Ben's neck went off without a hitch. He was still sleeping like a baby.

"Twenty minutes later, I was seated on a tree stump down by the stream. Countless thoughts raced through my head. I planned how I would lie in wait the next time the Englishman returned home and follow him and George to the barn when they went to take the food to the runaway slaves. Once they entered, I would sneak in behind and wait for them to open the trap door. Then I would show myself and act as if I had just discovered their deep dark secret."

Pop paused from his story-telling as Sam let out a long, loud yawn, then pulled out his pocket watch. "My goodness. Didn't realize it was so late. Well, I got to be getting home."

"What happened next?" I pleaded.

"That's another story," Pop replied. He and Sam stood and winked at each other.

It wasn't a coincidence that Uncle Sam yawned when he did; the winking gave him away. It was planned. Once again, I would be left hanging for another week.

# CHAPTER FIVE

A gentle pat on the shoulder brought me back into the present. I had been lost in my thoughts of days gone by; of days spent growing up with Pop; of countless hours spent listening to so many wonderful stories.

"He was a good man. We're all going to miss him, champ."

"Thank you Mr. Langford. Thanks for coming," was my reply to the man who had just offered his condolences. He addressed me as champ and that was an honor considering who he was. He was Sam Langford. Although he was a good number of years younger than Pop, Sam Langford was at one time a close friend of his and a frequent visitor to our house when I was younger and still living at home. After he patted my shoulder a couple more times, he walked past me up to Pop's casket and stood there a few minutes, staring down. I studied him as I had studied Pop earlier. It was he who was the champ, not me. Sam Langford was a former boxer. Pop had once told me that Sam Langford was, without a doubt, one of the most skilled boxers to ever climb into a ring. As far as Pop was concerned, Sam Langford should have been the boxing champion all those years that Jack Johnson held the title."

Sam was nicknamed the "Boston Tar Baby." He fought Johnson once when Johnson was a young fighter on his way to the top. The fight took place in Chelsea, Massachusetts, on April 26, 1906. Pop claimed to have been there seated in the third row from center ring. The first time Pop described the fight to me, I could tell that he was still angry about the final outcome.

"The house was packed," Pop began. "It looked like a mismatch if ever I saw one. Johnson, who weighed a good fifty pounds more than Langford, was by far the favorite to win the bout. But early in the fight, Langford surprised everyone, especially Jack Johnson. With a quick, powerful left hook to the jaw in the second round, Sam Langford knocked Johnson to the canvas. Jack Johnson stayed down until the count of nine before he managed to struggle back up. Funny thing was, it was the slowest counting that I ever heard. According to my watch, a damn accurate one it was, and the watches of the gentlemen sitting on both sides of me, Johnson was on the canvas for a good sixteen seconds. For the next thirteen rounds, Jack Johnson did what he had to do in order to avoid another one of the Boston Tar Baby's devastating left hooks.

"Johnson won by a decision, and I suspect at the same time, he decided that he never again wanted to tangle with Sam Langford because he refused to ever fight him again. Matter of fact, most of the boxers back then were afraid to go one-on-one with Sam in the ring. The only way Sam Langford could secure a fight with many of the leading white fighters was to sign what was termed a 'gentleman's agreement.' In plain English, he agreed to lose the fight. Although I don't admire the fact that he fought more fixed fights than any other boxer, I understand that he had to throw his fights in order to fight. Fact was, he could beat any boxer, black or white, that dared to climb in the ring with him."

The story Pop told me about Sam Langford that stood out the clearest in my mind was how one month before his sixteenth birthday, Sam fought two white men on the same night in Boston. It was the night of January 13, 1902, and when the back-to-back bouts were over, Sam had beaten both Jack Mc~lckar and William McDonald.

"The best fight I ever saw Sam fight was his bout with Joe Walcott on September 5, 1904, in Manchester, New Hampshire. Now that was a fight! The two of them slugged it out for fifteen rounds. Judge ruled it a draw. One of the best rulings I ever had the pleasure of hearing."

Sam Langford surprised me by showing up at the funeral. It had been years since I'd seen him. Once he retired from boxing he stopped coming around the house much.

I continued to study this once great boxer. His eyesight had all but failed him, and it was a known fact that he was impoverished. It wasn't a secret that he had been taken advantage of by his manager. Most of the Negro fighters during Sam's fighting days were exploited by their managers and their attorneys. Most of them were still being exploited.

Sam stood in silence in front of Pop's casket for a good five minutes before he turned away and made his way back down the aisle.

My eyes followed Sam Langford, better known as the Boston Tar Baby, until he took a seat in the last pew. I continued to look around. The church was almost filled to capacity with people from every walk of life. The sprinkling of white folks in the crowd surprised me somewhat because I didn't remember many ever coming to our home when I was young. It was true that a lot of Pop's business dealings were with them, but I never recalled him referring to any of them other than as business associates. A few of the white faces were familiar to me only because I had seen them in various newspapers or magazines.

Some of the most prominent Negroes of the day were in attendance. That didn't surprise me at all. Pop had lied in New York City for more than seventy years and was intimately involved in the Negro community. When he wasn't busy with his own affairs, he was attending one community meeting or another, or directly involved in helping those less fortunate than himself.

Charles Grant sat just a few rows in front of Sam Langford. I recognized him immediately. He was a long time friend of Pop's. The last time I had seen him was a few months before when he dropped by the house one Saturday afternoon while I was paying Pop a visit.

When I was younger, Charles Grant was a frequent visitor to the house and, on a few occasions, he would join Pop in his storytelling. It was from Charles Grant that I learned about the Negro Baseball League, and how it got started. Charles Grant was himself a former ball player in the League. In fact, he was the first Negro to sign with a white major league team. It was in 1901, when John J. McGraw, a baseball scout, saw Grant playing second base with the Columbia Giants while in Hot Springs, Arkansas. The Giants were a Negro baseball team from Chicago. McGraw was so impressed with Grant's skill as a ball player that he decided to sign him to play in the mayors.

Since Negroes were excluded from the majors, McGraw figured that if he passed him off as an Indian, then he could play. Grant was scheduled to play his first major league game in Chicago with the Baltimore team. His skills as a second baseman were well known to the Negro population of Chicago, and when he arrived at the stadium to play, the Negro women of Chicago showed up with bouquets of flowers for him. Once it became apparent that he was a Negro, he was released immediately from his contract.

It was Grant who first told me the history of the formation of the Negro Baseball League. "In 1867 the National Association for Baseball Players passed a resolution prohibiting Negroes from playing for any of the Association's teams. Negroes had no recourse except to start their own league. The first organized Negro baseball team was founded in 1885 in Babylon, Long Island, by Frank P. Thompson, the head waiter at the Argyle Hotel in New York. A white man named Walter Cook backed the team financially and named it the Cuban Giants. By 1887 there were seven clubs in the Negro League."

Pop was the one who told me about the first World Series held by the Negro League. It was held in New York in 1888. Teams from New York, Pittsburgh, Norfolk and Cuba participated in the series, which was won by the Cuban Giants of New York.

Seated next to Charles Grant was Carter G. Woodson, historian, author, editor and the founder of the Association for the Study of Afro American Life and History. I first met Carter Woodson back in 1914. He had come to the house to confer with Pop about establishing the Association. After the initial meeting between Woodson and Pop, they had several subsequent meetings prior to Woodson's founding of the Association for the Study of Afro-American Life in 1915.

There was at least one familiar or prominent person in each pew. Three rows in front of Carter G. Woodson sat several Negroes who were well known in the entertainment field. Charles Gilpin, who starred in The Emperor Jones, sat next to the aisle. To his immediate left was Florence Mills, a popular singer. To her left, were Noble Sissle and Eubie Blake, both were noted composers. Pop helped to finance one of the musicals that Blake, Sissle, and their partner Aubrey Lyles, wrote and in which Florence Mills starred.

In front of Eubie Blake was another long time friend of Pop's, William Mack Fetton. He and Pop had been friends as far back as I could remember. Fetton arrived in New York in 1901 and opened a repair shop fixing odds and ends. As the popularity of the automobile grew, Fetton began working on auto repairs. It wasn't long before he had his own garage. Shortly after that, Fetton opened an automobile repair school, one of the first in the country.

The most touching sight in the church was found in the first two rows to my left. Seated as erect as their aging bodies would let them, were a half dozen elderly Negro men dressed in their old, faded army uniforms. They were veterans of the Civil War who had served in the Massachusetts Fifty-fourth with Pop.

"Here it is sixty-four years since the end of the Civil War. I feel such a sense of pride watching these veterans of the war that helped abolish slavery sit proudly in their old, faded uniforms paying their last respects to one of their comrades" were my thoughts when my eyes fell upon the numerous medals collectively pinned to their uniforms. The sight of the medals took my thoughts back to the stories that Pop used to tell me of his days in the Union Army.

It was during one of his Saturday, stoop top, story-telling evenings that I first learned what it was like to be a Negro soldier during the Civil War.

One of the things that made Pop's stories so interesting was that he never just started telling a story without first giving a lot of background information relating to the actual story that he was about to tell.

Pop took great pride in the fact that he fought for the freedom of the rest of his people. The first time he shared stories of his soldiering days with me, he was quick to point out that the freedom of the slaves was not the primary reason for the war.

"Now don't get me wrong, President Lincoln was a good man and he truly believed that slavery was an evil thing, but he was more concerned with preserving the Union than he was with ending slavery. He wanted to avoid a war at all costs. If a workable compromise could have been agreed upon between the states which didn't allow slavery to exist within their borders, and the states which had become dependent upon slave labor, then there wouldn't have been an Emancipation Proclamation. At least not then," he added almost as an afterthought. "Matter of fact, well into the war, President Lincoln was still hoping to avoid having to end slavery by force.

"At President Lincoln's urging, Congress had gone as far as to pass a joint resolution agreeing to compensate slave-owners for the value of their slaves in any state adopting laws that gradually abolished slavery. Of course, none of the

Confederate states responded because in 1861 and 1862 the tides of war were favoring the Confederacy. It wasn't until after it became apparent that there weren't any takers for Congress' generous' offer that President Lincoln acted decisively on the issue of slavery.

"There were all sorts of laws passed and proposals put forth in an effort to avoid having to free all slaves unilaterally. Between December, 1860 and March of '61, several such proposals recommended that the Constitution be amended so as to deprive Congress of the power to abolish slavery. Another proposal suggested adding an amendment to the Constitution that would, in effect, bar slavery north of an imaginary line stretching from Norfolk, Virginia, to Wichita, Kansas. President Lincoln's home state of Illinois added an amendment to its constitution in 1862 which forbade mulattos from migrating or settling in the state."

"Was that law ever enforced?" I naively asked.

"Of course. They wouldn't have passed the law if they weren't going to enforce it. Before the law was made unconstitutional in 1865, a good number of mulattos were tried and convicted in Illinois courts for breaking the law. Since Illinois did not allow for slavery directly, the convicted mulattos were sold to the highest bidder in order to pay the large fines that were levied on them. Generally, the fines were so huge that it would have taken most of the mulattos the better part of their lifetime to pay them off through forced labor.

"If my memory serves me correctly," Pop continued, "It was sometime late in September of '62 that President Lincoln announced that as of January 1, 1863, slaves in the Confederate states or "the territory in rebellion," as Lincoln preferred to refer to the Confederacy, would be declared free. He went on to announce that slaveholders in states fighting on the side of the Union could keep their slaves or they could free them and be compensated by the Federal Government for each slave they freed.

"How to fix a price to pay owners for their slaves was a tricky question. However, slaveholders in Washington, D.C. received $300 for every adult slave they set free. When January 1, 1863, rolled around, slaves in Alabama, Arkansas, Florida, Georgia, Louisiana, Mississippi, North Carolina, South Carolina, Virginia and Texas were technically set free. Mind you, I say technically because there was still the matter of the war that was being fought. The Union had to win the war if the Emancipation Proclamation was going to be worth anything other than the paper that it was printed on. I don't have to tell you that the slaveholders in the Confederate states didn't go around announcing to their slaves that Mr. Lincoln had declared them free. Still, slaves found out about their newly declared freedom by way of the grapevine telegraph."

"What was the grapevine telegraph?" I quickly asked.

Pop cut his eyes at me briefly, which was something he did when he wanted to let me know that he had been anticipating my question, before he continued with his storytelling without so much as missing a breath.

"The grapevine telegraph was a code consisting of signals that had been first used by members of the Underground Railroad. Different numbers of straws hanging from the mouth meant one thing; the manner in which a cap was tilted on a slave's head meant something else. A variety of such almost unnoticeable antics, combined with numerous hand signals, provided an effective means of silent communication.

In addition to the silent signals, slaves had worked out an elaborate system of code names for just about everything and everyone."

A coughing sound from one of the veterans seated in the church momentarily interrupted my remembrance of Pop's war days. Again, I looked at the medals on their chests and drifted back to the events, remembering as if it were yesterday.

"Ever since the start of the war, there were those who felt it would bring about the end of slavery," Pop informed Helen and me.

"Most of the Negro leaders at the time were angered by the fact that Negroes weren't allowed to join the Union Army and help fight for the freedom of their people. Arguments concerning the merits of having Negro soldiers could be heard wherever Negroes gathered. Many felt that freedom won at the hand of white blood only, wasn't real freedom. When the Emancipation Proclamation was read, it gave Negroes that had been advocating for the right to join in the fight against the Confederacy additional reason to rejoice. One sentence in the Proclamation declared that free and freed Negroes would be allowed to join the Union forces.'"

"How many of us joined up?" I asked. "Now hold on there a minute," was Pop's immediate reply. "It wasn't quite that simple. You see, the decision to use Negroes as soldiers didn't necessarily come about because of any broad humanitarian resolve on the part of President Lincoln or the Congress. It came about largely out of the realities of war. It didn't take much thinking to conclude that the Confederate army was going to kill a great many more Union soldiers before the war ended, one way or another. The popular thinking was that a good number of white men could avoid getting killed if a large enough number of those soldiers were Colored troops.

"White soldiers talked about Negroes being allowed to serve openly. 'A Negro can stop a bullet just as well as a white man,' they chanted. 'For every Negro killed in battle, one more white man will get to return home to his family and friends at the war's end,' they would often add. Toward the end of January, the War Department authorized Governor John Andrew of Massachusetts to establish a regiment of Negro troops.

"Not every Negro leader felt that Negroes should be so quick to enlist. Some leaders wanted a few questions answered before they would serve as recruiting agents for the Union Army. What would be the status of Colored soldiers? Would they be allowed to fight? If so, who would lead them in combat? It had been rumored that Colored troops could best serve the Union Army as laborers and teamsters. The stipulation that all commissioned officers in the Negro regiment must be white didn't sit well with most Negro leaders. Then there was the question of pay. It was made clear that Colored troops were to be paid less than white troops. Just how strong some Negroes felt about these and several other issues concerning Negro service in the Union Army was made clear in April of the same year.

"Fredrick Douglass was one of the recruiting officers for the Union. On April 27, 1863, while making a speech right here in New York City, in an attempt to sign up Negro recruits, Douglass was interrupted by a Mr. Robert Johnson. Johnson, like Douglass, was himself quite an eloquent and forceful speaker. Johnson gave a rousing speech, appealing to all the potential Colored recruits gathered, not to volunteer to serve in the Union army, unless colored soldiers were guaranteed the same pay and rights accorded white soldiers.

"Before Robert Johnson spoke, quite a few of us gathered at the rally had been more than anxious to sign up. By the time he finished speaking and turned the platform back over to Fredrick Douglass, it was an entirely different story. Fredrick Douglass' efforts resulted in only one of us young, able, free Negroes present signing up that day.

"Although Robert Johnson was quite effective with his speech, that wasn't what made me delay signing up that day. After Johnson spoke and Mr. Douglass made his second appeal, an older gentleman standing next to me started addressing me. 'No Sir, even if I was young enough to sign up, I wouldn't. Mr. Lincoln don't want us here no way. Weren't but a couple of weeks ago he was still signing deals to ship us back to Africa,' the stranger reminded me.

"He had given me something to think about. What he said was in fact partially true. Whether Mr. Lincoln wanted us here or not was questionable; that he favored returning Negroes to Africa and the West Indies was a documented fact."

"What do you mean?" I asked almost in shock, for I hadn't heard or read anything about any plan of Abraham Lincoln's to send Negroes back to Africa.

Pop stared at me for a couple of seconds before responding. "There's a lot of history concerning colored folks that you haven't heard about, and you won't read about as long as white folks are writing their history books. Now if you want to hear about Mr. Lincoln's plan hush up and listen."

"Yes Sir, I'm all ears."

"You said a mouthful there," Helen added jokingly as she reached over and tugged on my ears.

"Let's see, where was I?" Pop said in a tone that let us know he was ready to continue without further interruptions. "The elderly gentleman's reference to Mr. Lincoln not wanting us here reminded me of what he was referring to. He was alluding to something that happened in August of '62. Shortly after Mr. Lincoln issued his Emancipation Proclamation, good old Abe Lincoln announced his grand colonization plan for American Negroes.

"Immediate protests over Lincoln's plan were launched by Negro leaders, but to no avail. Encouraged by Mr. Lincoln, Congress allocated more than a half million dollars for the first installment on Lincoln's colonization plan. It was estimated that the total project would cost more than twenty million dollars.

"A contract to begin carrying out the colonization plan was signed with a white adventurer named Bernard Kock. Kock leased an island off the Hatian coast called Vache and agreed to colonize five thousand Negroes. The contract was cancelled when it was later discovered that Bernard Kock had no intention of transporting anyone to Vache. Instead, he had planned to hand over the Negroes entrusted to his care to a Confederate privateer named Captain Semmes. I needn't tell you that Captain Semmes' only intention was to return the Negroes to slavery in the South.

"Now you would think that would have been enough to encourage Lincoln to abandon his pet project. Well it wasn't. Just a few weeks before the rally in New York to recruit Negroes for the Union Army, a new deal had been struck with several white businessmen to once again carry out Lincoln's plan. Matter of fact, it was a day or two before the rally that somewhere around 450 Negroes boarded a ship named the Ocean Ranger and were on their way to Vache. Once I was reminded of that, I decided that I'd better take a few days to think about signing up."

"How many more of us settled in Vache," I asked out of a deep desire to know. The whole idea of Lincoln's colonization plan amazed and flabbergasted me.

"None to be exact," was Pop's initial answer.

"What happened to the colony?" I inquired further.

Pop slowly shook his head, then continued. "You know I like to keep my stories in proper order. Now how can I tell you what happened to the colony if it didn't happen yet in my story?" Pop teased. "It wasn't until more than a year later that I learned what happened to the colony and most of those unfortunate enough to have gone there. I suppose though, it won't hurt to get a little ahead of myself.

"Lincoln and his backers in Congress were so anxious to carry out their colonization plan that accommodations such as housing, schools or medical facilities had not been provided for the colonists on Vache. Once they arrived on the island the 'settlers' were forced to construct shelters out of what was available. That meant thatched, crude palm-covered huts. Kock of all people was sent along as governor of the colony, adding insult to injury."

"Although Kock's position carried very little authority, he made such a nuisance of himself that he was run off the island. In December of the same year, Lincoln sent an agent to to investigate the conditions on Vache. When the agent, D.C. Donnohue, arrived, close to half the Negro colonists were dead.

"Three months later, based in part on Donnohue's recommendation, Lincoln was forced to bring the surviving Negroes back to the United States. Lincoln's dream for colonizing Negroes outside the American continent was laid to rest on July 2, 1864, when Congress repealed the Negro Deportation Bill."

"Unbelievable," I whispered to Helen, trying not to interrupt Pop again.

Pop had the sharpest set of ears of anyone I knew. He heard my whisper and responded accordingly. "Believe me. Every word of it's true. Well anyway, I mulled that and a few other things over in my mind before deciding to sign up for service with the Massachusetts Fifty-fourth on April 30th.

"Now, as was to be expected, the Confederacy didn't take too kindly to the idea of the Union Army sending Negro troops into battle against them. They let it be known that colored enlisted men who were captured would not be treated as ordinary prisoners of war. Of course, this didn't bother any of us Negro soldiers much because we didn't expect any mercy from the Confederates, if they captured us anyway."

"Did you get to do any fighting Pop?" I interrupted, asking with all the curiosity of an eleven year old.

"Did I do any fighting? Why less than two months after I signed up with the 54th, I was in the thick of battle. We spent all of May and most of June learning about soldiering before we marched south. It wasn't long before I saw more action than I wanted to see. But before I tell you about that, let me tell you a little about our regiment.

"Our commanding officer was Colonel Robert G. Shawl I knew all about him, or I should say I knew all about his family before I signed up, because his grandfather had been at that meeting I told you about on the farm back in '56. The Colonel's family were well-known northerners and his grandfather was one of the leading Abolitionists before the war. All the officers attached to the 54th Regiment were white, and if there was any prejudice in them, it didn't show. They treated us like I suspect they would have treated any soldier under their command. We got to know each other pretty well.

"In July of '63 we received orders that we were to be the leading element of a planned attack on Fort Wagner, a Confederate fort on the South Carolina seacoast. Word was that the fort was well-manned and it wouldn't be too easy. We were told that after our initial assault, regiments of white soldiers would follow up our attack.

"We marched almost continuously for three days and nights with no sleep, and without food for the last two days of the march. Finally, we were in position about three-quarters of a mile from the fort, all six hundred of us.

"On July 18th, while we waited for dark to fall and our attack to begin, we talked among ourselves. We knew that how we fared in battle that day would have a lot to do with how the Union Army used colored soldiers for the remainder of the war Mostly, I talked with Charles and Lewis Douglass,

Fredrick Douglass' sons. I had known them for a few years, and felt secure knowing that they would be charging into battle with me.

"It was close to eight in the evening when darkness fell and the order to charge the fort was given. We advanced within two hundred yards before the Confederates opened fire on us. They hit us with everything they had. Shells from their cannons exploded all around us and countless bullets from their rifles whistled through the air. Men fell dead and wounded all around me. Still, despite our heavy losses, we pushed on. We were fighting for the entire Negro race. If anything, we sped up our advance towards the fort. Our officers were at the front and led us on until finally we came upon a huge ditch, which momentarily halted our advance.

"There was a colored Sergeant, name of William H. Carney who really inspired us. He had already been shot twice, but when we stopped, he planted the flag he had been carrying right at the top of the ditch, for all to see. Then before we could catch our breath good, Colonel Shaw stood up in front of us, raised his sword, and shouted, 'Forward, Fifty-fourth'. He didn't get to lead us on the charge because an enemy bullet went straight through his heart, killing him instantly.

"Led by our other officers, we charged on without Colonel Shawl Before we reached the fort, several more of our officers had been killed or wounded, along with hundreds of the fighting men of the 54th. Those of us who managed to get inside the fort weren't able to hold it because by then our numbers had been greatly reduced and Fort Wagner was better defended than anyone had thought. The Confederates pushed us back into the night. Those of us who could, continued to fight. When additional troops finally arrived to reinforce us, they were beaten back, too.

"The Confederates were outraged by the fact that Negro troops, led by white officers, had dared to attack them. As a display of their anger and what they thought was an insult to all Union officers and Shaw's family, the Confederates first stripped Colonel Shaw's uniform from his body, then threw it in a ditch filled with dead colored soldiers and covered it.

"It didn't work out quite the way they planned it. It was a month after the initial battle for Fort Wagner when Union troops finally captured the fort, and a search was begun for the Colonel's body. The Army wanted to return it to New York for burial. When the Colonel's father heard about the army's plans for his son's body, he fired off a letter to the commanding officer of the Union Army at Fort Wagner, requesting that his son's grave not be disturbed. The letter was read to those of us who had fought alongside the Colonel. It made us even prouder than we already were to have served under his command. Mr. Shaw's letter read in part, 'A soldier's most appropriate burial place is on the field where he has fallen. I shall therefore be much obliged if you would prevent the disturbance of his remains or those buried with him'.

"The manner in which we fought and the countless acts of bravery and heroism displayed by us at Fort Wagner left no doubt that the Negro was as fine a soldier as had ever put on a uniform.

"By the end of October of '63 there were fifty-eight regiments of Negro troops numbering more than 37,000 men. By the end of the war, more than 186,000 Negroes had served in the Union Army.

"Sergeant Carney later received the Congressional Medal of Honor for heroism displayed at the battle of Fort Wagner. He was one of fourteen Negro soldiers to receive the Congressional Medal of Honor during the Civil War. Lots of other men of the 54th received decorations for individual acts of bravery during the ill-fated attack on Fort Wagner.

"Mind you, all our battles weren't fought on the battlefield. We had proven ourselves equal to any soldier on either side, but there was still the question of unequal treatment as soldiers. We were paid $10 per month plus $3 clothing allowance, while white soldiers were paid $13 a month plus $3.50 clothing allowance. Well you know your grandpop. I wasn't one to tolerate what I felt was an injustice, so I organized a protest of sorts among the men of the 54th. While we were still in South Carolina, we refused to accept any monies at all, until Washington officially made our rate of pay equal to the white soldiers."

"Did you ever have any second thoughts about having fought in the war, Pop?" I asked inquisitively, when he paused to catch his breath.

Pop leaned back and ran his hand up and down his chin. Whenever he did that, I knew I had asked a question that would produce a most interesting response.

"Not exactly. But there was a point in the war when I wished that I could have been back home defending the Negroes of New York City from vicious white mobs."

"When was that?" I interrupted.

"Relax, Goldie, I'm getting to that. In March of '63 the Union passed a national conscription law. The new draft law wasn't very popular. There was a clause which didn't sit too well with the common man. It provided that anyone who was drafted, but could pay three hundred dollars or could offer another person in their place, was exempt from military service. Of course, the wealthy were able to either pay the three hundred dollars or pay someone to act as a substitute in order to keep their sons out of the war.

"The first selection of those to be drafted took place in New York on Saturday, July 11, a week before the battle of Fort Wagner. By Monday morning, street protests over the draft were in full swing. White folks marched up and down Seventh and Eighth Avenues shouting slogans like, 'Down with the police' and 'Away with the draft'. Soon, however, the mob diverted its focus from attacks on the police to attacks on Negroes. You see, many of the rioters now believed that the main reason for the war was the abolition of slavery and not the preservation of the Union. Agitators among the mob convinced the massive crowd to breakup into smaller groups and go on a nigger hunt.

"After quickly dispersing into smaller groups, the rioters set out. They spread across Manhattan and began beating and lynching any Negro they ran across. None was spared from the vicious white mobs. Negro men, women, children, infants, and the elderly all fell victim to the mob's violence. The mob raided various businesses known to employ Negroes, and dragged the Negroes, who were unfortunate enough to be at work, out into the streets where they were beaten. In many cases, after they were whipped they were hung from lampposts. Several blocks where Negroes lived were burned to the ground. The police weren't much help because their own lives were in constant danger.

"The viciousness of the mobs reached a new low when they attacked the Colored Orphan Asylum. It was that attack, more than anything else, that made me want to desert the 54th; at least long enough to return home and seek revenge on the attackers."

"What was the Colored Orphan Asylum?" I asked.

"It was a four story brick structure down on Fifth Avenue between Forty-third and Forty-fourth Streets which housed more than twelve hundred Negro orphans all under the age of twelve. From newspaper accounts that reached us in South Carolina, I was able to piece this much together about what went on before the attack on the orphanage.

"Rioting had been going on all around the asylum. Expecting the worse, the superintendent barricaded the doors before the inevitable arrival of the rioters. The children watched in fear from the windows as-the violent, angry mob closed in. Before the mob could break down the front doors, the superintendent, assisted by his staff, snuck the orphans out a rear door and hurriedly led them to relative safety in a nearby police station. Along the way, the children couldn't help but see the dozens of mob victims hanging from lampposts or lying in the streets.

"The orphans had barely made it out of the building when the mob battered down the front doors and charged into the building with axes and hatchets in hand. Once inside, they began destroying the place. Unknown to the superintendent and his staff, a little girl had been left behind in the hurried exodus to safety. Members of the mob found her curled up under a bed. They dragged her out and killed her. Then the rioters looted the building, taking anything that they thought was of value, including toys left behind by the children. When they were finished looting, the rioters set the inside of the building on fire.

"The orphans spent the next three days and nights barricaded in the police station, surviving on the little food that was smuggled in by several priests from a nearby church. On the fourth day, soldiers arrived and with fixed bayonets, escorted the horrified children past a screaming, blood thirsty, ugly mob. The frightened, hungry and tired orphans were taken to Blackwell Island where they spent the next three months.

"When news of that raid on the Colored Orphan Asylum reached us, a bunch of us wanted to desert and return to New York and seek revenge against the 'good white' citizens of New York City. That was the closest that I came to regretting that I was in the Army. Mind you, it wasn't being in the Army. It was just that I wasn't in New York during the riots. There probably wouldn't have been much I could have done to change things, and I suspect it was that reasoning which made it easy for me not to desert."

There were a good many other stories that Pop and a few of his friends who had served in the 54th with him had shared with me. Before I could recall anymore, of them, the minister entered the church, walked over to me, and interrupted my thoughts.

"We're ready to begin the services. Will you be delivering the eulogy?"

"No Reverend, Sam Harris will," I replied as I looked to my left at Sam, who appeared to be lost deep in his own thoughts.

A few minutes later, the service was under way. Sam delivered a eulogy that accurately described Pop's life and outlook. He concluded his tribute to Pop with three sentences that basically said it all.

"Joseph Cinque Covington was always proud of his skin color. He was faithful, yet defiant towards a country that at times treated him as less than a man. Although he often expressed bitterness towards the injustices endured by all Negro Americans, he never stopped believing in the eventual achievement of equal opportunity and justice for all Americans without regard to the color of their skin."

**T**he service took an hour to complete. When it was over, I sat in silence, awed at the number of prominent people who had filed past Pop's casket. As I watched the mourners, I couldn't help but remember when Pop finally got around to continuing the story of how he first discovered what the big secret was around the farm.

Several weeks had passed since Pop revealed to Helen, Sam and me how he slipped the key from around Ben's neck and made his discovery of the room hidden beneath the stall in the barn. Business necessitated that he leave town for a couple of weeks, and it was a most agonizing two weeks for me. I desperately wanted to know what happened when he confronted the Englishman with his discovery. Pop was an expert at ending his stories at a point that left you thirsting for more.

The summer days were carefree ones for me, and although it was a chore deciding what I could do to pass the time away, there was never a lack of choices. After a little persuading, Helen agreed to let me spend a few days visiting with my classmate and good friend, Butch Lewis. Since Butch's father was a friend of Pop's, and Helen knew his mother quite well from church, Helen felt I would be under eyes just as watchful as hers while I was visiting Butch's family.

Mr. Lewis owned several grocery stores and earned a good income. He was fond of reminding everyone that he made his money in the Negro community and that was where he chose to live. In reality, it had been just a little more than a year since the Lewis family moved from around the corner from us, to the heart of one of the city's most infamous Negro neighborhoods, San Juan Hill on West Sixty-third Street.

For the most part, West Sixty-third and the surrounding blocks, which made up the Hill, consisted of old rundown three and four-story tenement houses. What Mr. Lewis didn't voluntarily tell anyone, when he bragged about how he lived among his people, was that the Lewis family lived in a spacious apartment in the Philip Houses, which was comparable to living in the lap of luxury. The buildings were around five years old and had been built as model apartments. Although only six stories high, they towered over the surrounding dilapidated housing stock. Besides excellent maintenance, the houses had beautiful rooftop gardens and were steam heated; a luxury almost unknown in any other Negro or poor neighborhoods in the city.

The best part about going to spend a few days with Butch was that Mr. Lewis picked me up in his shiny new Ford Model T. Butch and his father arrived for me bright and early on Saturday morning I had been up for several hours, anxiously waiting for them. When Mr. Lewis knew that Pop wasn't home, he didn't get out of his car. Instead, he would honk the horn several times, signaling me of their arrival. He did this, actually, to annoy Helen. For some unexplained reason she couldn't stand the sound the car horn made. One day she made the mistake of letting Mr. Lewis know that the honking annoyed her to no end. Me, I didn't need a signal announcing their arrival because I could see them when they pulled up, from where I stood in the parlor, with my face pressed against the window.

It seemed like forever between the time they arrived and when I was finally able to dash out of the house. Before I could leave, I had to listen to Helen's seemingly endless list of dos and don'ts.

"Don't forget to be on your best manners. Don't get on Isabel's nerves. Don't go wandering around the neighborhood, or get into any fights with those ruffians down there. Be sure to say your prayers at night, be on your best behavior; brush your teeth before you go to bed, and wash your face and hands before you sit down to eat." On and on she went for what seemed like hours. What Helen didn't know was that by the time she was on her third don't, my mind was already on its way to the Hill. When at last she was done, Helen handed me a bag and instructed me, "Tell Isabel that I baked this potato pie especially for her. Now hold it up flat. Don't tilt the bag. You have fun."

"Yes, Ma'am. I will."

Before Helen could think of anything else to tell me to remember to do or don't do, I snatched my suitcase up with my free hand, dashed out the door and down the steps.

"Careful with that pie!" Helen shouted. I looked back in time to see her shaking her clenched fist at Mr. Lewis.

"Good morning Helen. Lovely day isn't it?" He shouted at her as I climbed into the car beside Butch.

A few minutes later, we were speeding beneath the Broadway elevated train, pretending that we were racing the other cars we passed along the way to the Hill. In reality, we were doing anything but racing. We couldn't have been traveling more than fifteen miles an hour.

After we arrived at their apartment building and parked the car, Mr. Lewis raced Butch and I up the stairs. He beat us in enough time to open the apartment door before we reached it. Once inside, I greeted Butch's mother.

"Good morning, Mrs. Lewis."

"Good morning, Goldie."

"Helen sent this potato pie for you. She said to tell you that she baked it especially for you."

"Why thank you." Mrs. Lewis reached out as I handed her the bag containing the pie.

"If you three boys behave yourself today, maybe I'll let each of you have a piece after supper," she said, smiling teasingly at Mr. Lewis.

"I hope you brought a hearty appetite with you, Goldie. I whipped up a stack of buckwheats especially for you."

"Yes Ma'am," I answered before licking my lips and rubbing my stomach. Butch's mom made the best buckwheat pancakes of anyone in town, and plenty of them. She always seemed glad to have me visiting and always had breakfast waiting for us.

"Go on and put Goldie's suitcase in the room. The two of you go wash your hands and hurry back before things get cold." It didn't take Butch and me much time to carry out his mother's instructions.

During breakfast, when I was sure no one was watching, I stared at Mrs. Lewis. She was a very pretty woman and always seemed so cheerful. Whenever I saw her, I imagined that wherever my mother was, she was just as pretty and cheerful.

Butch and I stuffed ourselves until we almost burst, then excused ourselves and headed downstairs to play. A short while later, his father came down and joined us in a game of stoopball. Mr. Lewis was no more than thirty-five years old and always seemed so full of energy. Although I loved Pop dearly and never wished to have been raised by anyone else, at times when I was with Butch and his father, I was a bit envious of Butch because his father was young enough to play with him and his friends.

When we finished our game of stoop ball, Mr. Lewis went to check on his stores. The remainder of the morning passed quickly. It was a few minutes past noon when Mrs. Lewis called us upstairs for lunch. After lunch, Butch and I went outside to play some more.

By late afternoon, several other boys from the neighborhood had joined us in a game of marbles. One of the fellows playing with us was named Ronnie. Butch had spoken to me about him and undoubtedly had spoken to him about me. Butch told me that Ronnie was the king of the Hill when it came to playing the dozens and that nobody could out-rank him. Butch had his reasons for telling me. In my neighborhood, I was the king and Butch figured that when I met Ronnie, I wouldn't be able to resist challenging him to a game of the dozens. Butch was right because shortly after Ronnie joined us, I issued him a challenge.

"Butch told me that you're the dozens champ around here."

"Around here! I'm the best in New York, in the country, in the world," Ronnie bragged

"Well I'm not saying you're not, but I am saying that you've got the ugliest face that I ever did see. I bet your face could stop a clock."

The challenge was on. Part of the strategy in winning at the dozens was slipping in the-first good crack. If you did that successfully, the crowd boosted you on.

"Good one, Goldie," Butch cheered.

"You gonna, take that, Ronnie?" another boy chimed in.

It was understood that Ronnie wasn't going to take it.

By the look on his face, I knew it was going to be a good match. Ronnie stood there for a good minute, looking me up and down. Slowly, he began to crack a smile. I braced myself for his comeback remark while I thought of my next crack.

If you were a good dozens player, you had to think ahead to your next crack before your opponent let loose with his. You also had to be quick at spontaneous cracks because if the person gave you a lead-in, based on their crack, you had to take advantage of it.

There weren't any rules on what you could or couldn't say. It was however, understood that if you chose to talk about someone's mother, you did so at great risk. You could say anything you wanted about your opponent's father, brothers or sisters. You could call him anything from a baboon sipping vinegar to a drip lip platypus, and it was taken in the spirit of the game. But if you cracked on a person's mother, you risked the verbal fight escalating into a fistfight. It didn't matter how good a fighter you were. When a person got angry with you for talking bad about his mother, the person usually just started acting as if they had a sudden attack of lunacy. Even if you won the fight, you would remember having been in one for a long time. So, cracks on mothers were out.

Our game of the dozens went on for a good two full hours. Ronnie was a much better dozens player than I thought he would be. My skill at playing the dozens surprised him as much as his had surprised me. Once it became apparent that neither of us would out-rank the other, we decided to call it a draw for the day. We agreed to go at it again later in the week.

The remainder of the week passed quickly. My rematch at the dozens with Ronnie ended in a second draw. We decided to share the title. After all, our neighborhoods were worlds a part so we figured that there was room for two kings of the dozens in New York City.

Mr. Lewis drove me home late Friday afternoon. The following seven days seemed to take forever to pass. Pop returned early Saturday morning while I was still asleep. When he woke me up, I sprung out of bed genuinely glad to see him. Whenever Pop went away on business, deep down inside I feared that he too would leave me like my mother did. Only when he returned would the fear subside. Breakfast went just as every other Saturday morning meal.

Pop turned the kitchen into a disaster area and when Helen arrived on the scene, she threw her usual fit. After breakfast, Pop had to leave to attend a meeting of what he called the Harmony Group, an informal organization of American Negro, Puerto Rican, Hatian, British West Indian businessmen, and community leaders. The focus of the group was to find ways of promoting peace and harmony between the four minority groups.

Although the Bureau of Immigration lumped all four groups together under the category of African Black, there was very little, if any, unity among the various groups. The Hatians associated more with American Negroes than did the British West Indians or Puerto Ricans. The British West Indian saw himself as more ambitious than the American Negro and resented being called a Negro. Most of them clung to their British citizenship and British attitudes. Prejudice was rampant between the native Negro population of New York and the West Indian immigrants.

There was a rift between the native Negro population and the Spanish speaking population of New York, but it wasn't as openly expressed as was the one between the West Indian population and the native Negro population. That was, in part, because there was very little social contact between Spanish speaking people and native Negroes. Even though, in most cases, they lived in Negro communities, the Spanish speaking population wanted nothing to do with Negroes. It didn't take them long after arrival in the city to realize that white Americans put immigrants who spoke a foreign language into a separate class from natives Negroes. Most Spanish speaking immigrants considered themselves white, regardless of whether or not they were as dark as the darkest Negro in town.

Pop always returned home from those meetings frustrated. He would say, "The white man's got us all where he wants us: Divided! And we're doing a good job of making sure we stay that way.

Normally, on rainy Saturdays, either I spent the afternoon at Herby's house or he came over to ours. Since Herby was visiting with his relatives in North Carolina, I was left to fend for myself. Helen was her usual helpful self, quick to suggest something for me to do.

"I've been after you all week to give your room a good cleaning. Seems like the perfect thing to do on a rainy day."

"Yes Ma'am," I replied reluctantly.

It didn't take me long to clean my room. After I put everything away, I decided to read a book. I enjoyed reading. In a way, I looked forward to rainy days on the weekend because ultimately, I would find time to curl up on my bed with one of the many books from our well-stocked library.

Finally, after selecting a book on famous Negro freedom fighters, I returned to the quiet of my room. Book in hand, I stretched out on the bed and made myself comfortable. I spent the remainder of the afternoon alongside freedom fighter after freedom fighter, helping them in their quest to end slavery and establish equal rights for Negroes. The sound of Helen's voice summoning me interrupted my adventures.

"Supper's ready, Goldie. Hurry on down."

"Coming!" I shouted.

The book had been most enjoyable and I didn't really want to put it down. But I knew that when Helen called, she meant for me to come right then. So, I stuck a piece of paper in the book to mark my place, slammed it shut, placed it on my nightstand and headed down the hall to the bathroom to wash my hands. The first thing that Helen would ask me when I got downstairs was, "Did you wash up?" Lots of things about her were predictable.

Sure enough, before I stepped off the last step, she called out from the kitchen, "Did you wash up before coming downstairs?"

"Yes, Ma'am." I wanted to avoid her inspecting my hands. No matter how much I scrubbed them, Helen always commented that they still looked dirty to her, so I went straight into the dining room. Much to my delight Pop and Sam were already seated at the table laughing- about something. Immediately upon seeing me, their laughter turned into mild chuckles. Sam spoke first. "Hi there. Didn't think you were going to come out of your room until tomorrow sometime."

"Hi Pop. Hi Uncle Sam. When did you get here? I didn't here the bell ring."

"That's because it didn't. I ran into your uncle coming out of the bakery on my way home," Pop interjected. "I called upstairs, but you didn't answer. We've been here for a good hour."

"What were you and Pop laughing about a minute ago?"

"Nothing. Nothing at all," Sam answered, glanced over at Pop, then turned his head back toward me.

"Now why you want to fib to the child, Sam Harris. You know good and well what we were laughing about. You gonna tell him or am I?"

"You tell him, since you're the one who was laughing the hardest."

"If you insist. It'll be my pleasure. Right after I bumped into your uncle, we were walking down Eighth Avenue, and a skinny, pale, ugly gal came prancing up to him and started blabbing on about how it wasn't very nice of him not to keep the promise he made two weeks ago to visit her again.

Your uncle looked the woman right in the eyes and said with the straightest face imaginable, I beg your pardon,' really uppity like, 'I'm afraid that you must have me confused with someone else.' Well, she was real cool about it. The woman stepped back, looked Sam up and down and replied in a more uppity tone than Sam used, 'I beg your pardon. I must have made a mistake, Sam Harris.' Then without saying another word, she strolled away.

Right before you came in, your uncle over there was still trying to convince me that he hadn't ever seen the woman before in his life. I was reminding him that I saw her lots of times before and so did he. She works over at Smalls, and you know it, Sam Harris."

"Still, say I don't remember seeing her before. And I didn't know what she was referring to about visiting her again, considering the fact that I never visited her in the first place."

"Come on, Sam. You can tell me. I won't tell anyone else. Spent a little time with her a couple of weeks ago, hey Sam?" Pop teased as he nodded his head and gave Sam a quick wink.

"Don't remember ever seeing her at Smalls, and I certainly ain't spent no time with her alone."

"Well tell me, how did she know your name?

"Lucky guess," Sam replied, trying to keep a straight face. Before Pop could say anything else, Helen entered the dining room carrying part of our supper.

"I'll help you carry the rest in," I volunteered.

"That's okay, I can manage it alone. Sam brought a chocolate cake for dessert," she added on her way back into the kitchen.

You couldn't put much over on Helen. It was almost as if she could read minds. She knew that I had volunteered to help her in the kitchen because I wanted to see what Uncle Sam bought from the bakery.

"She got your number good that time," Pop commented.

During supper, Pop repeated his story to Helen and she agreed with him. "Sam knew the woman alright." Sam stuck fast to his denial.

Fifty minutes after we began eating, we were finished. Helen and I cleared the table and went to clean up the kitchen. The rain hadn't let up all day. In fact, judging by the sound of it beating against the back of the house, it was pouring harder than ever. The weather ruled out sitting outside, so Pop and Sam went into the living room.

The chimes of the grandfather clock rang out just as Helen and I joined them. It was seven p.m. It had been a long two weeks, but the waiting would soon be over. I watched as Pop leaned back in his favorite chair, crossed his legs, and cleared his throat. He took one last long draw on his cigar, put it out, and slowly blew out the smoke.

"I suspect you've been anxiously waiting for me to continue where I left off with my story," he said, looking directly at me and winking.

"Go on with your story. Bad enough we had to wait two weeks to find out what happened after you figured out that your farm was a stopover for the Underground Railroad," Helen instructed him.

In my readings earlier that day, I had learned all about the Underground Railroad, so I listened with renewed interest as Pop began.

"After I discovered the hidden room in the barn, months passed without anything happening. The Englishman came and went in his usual manner, except that he arrived during the daytime and while home, normal amounts of food were prepared. I had decided to wait until I was sure that the room was full of passengers on the Railroad to confront him with my find. Keeping my secret was almost unbearable. Still, I kept silent about my find, lest I'd have to explain how I got into the barn in the first place. The only way I could get around that was to slip in the barn the very next night the Englishman and Chester were escorting the runaway slaves to their hiding place, then confront them as if I had just discovered what they were up to.

"Five months passed before I saw signs that something was about to happen. It was the second weekend in January. The Englishman returned to the farm after being away since the day after Christmas. During the next two days, numerous meetings took place between Chester, George, and him in Chester's cabin. On several occasions, I snuck up beside the cabin and pressed my ear against the outside wall in an attempt to hear what they were talking about. I didn't have any success because whenever they met in the cabin that weekend, they spoke in hushed and guarded tones.

"Early Monday morning, the Englishman left the farm to return to the city. Whatever they had planned was a big secret. My immediate thoughts centered around the secret room. But I quickly brushed those thoughts aside. Things just didn't point in that direction because on the other occasions that I figured out runaway slaves had been harbored in the barn, there weren't a bunch of secret meetings preceding their arrival.

"It wasn't until Wednesday that I first got hints as to what was going on. By chance, I entered the kitchen just in time to hear George commenting to Chester, 'Lord, I don't reckon there has ever been so many important Negroes together in one place as there's gonna be here come Saturday.' It was obvious that neither of them was expecting me. My unanticipated appearance in the doorway produced a dead silence.

"Are we having company this weekend?"

"Boy, I done told you about always sneaking around," George blurted out in an angry voice.

"I wasn't sneaking around. I live here. Seems to me that everyone's been sneaking around here, except me,' I shouted back.

"Don't you go and get sassy with me, young man. Now what you mean by that remark?'

Chester remained silent. I continued my verbal exchange with George as I stared at Chester, and he stared back at me.

"All I meant was that there has been an awful lot of whispering going on here behind closed doors lately. And now I hear you saying something about some important visitors on Saturday. I'm not a kid anymore. I know a lot more about what's going on around this place than anyone thinks I do."

My last remark just sort of rolled off my tongue before I realized what I was saying. Chester broke eye contact with me and turned toward George. The concern was evident on their faces as they both turned their attention on me.

"Ain't nothin going on around here that concerns you, until Mr. Covington decides it concerns you. I don't know what you do or don't know. Don't rightly want to know, either. I'll give you a piece of good advice, though. If you know something that you ain't supposed to know, you best keep it to yourself," George replied in a manner which let me know that it was more than a suggestion. While George spoke, Chester just stood there shaking his head from side to side.

"So who's coming here Saturday?" I boldly persisted.

"Your father will be back on Friday. Why don't you ask him?"

For the first time in my life, George referred to the Englishman as my father. I was numbed and momentarily lost for words.

"What's the matter, cat got ya tongue? Ya was full of sass a moment ego," Chester added.

"I will ask him!" was all I shouted before turning away and running out of the room.

"The attic was my sanctuary. In the dark and quiet that surrounded me, I tried to figure out who the important people were that were coming to the house on Saturday. It was obvious there was a definite purpose for such a gathering. It didn't take much for me to conclude that the meeting had something to do with the Underground Railroad, and whoever was coming to the farm was involved with the abolitionists movement in one way or another.

"The house was a beehive of activity on Thursday and Friday. Every nook and cranny was thoroughly cleaned. Cots, which I suspected were taken from the secret room beneath the barn, were placed in the bedrooms to accommodate the expected guests. That led me to conclude that many people were expected. The excitement mounted in me as Saturday drew near. If my assumption was correct, I would get to see and meet many of the famous freedom fighters I had been reading about over the past several years.

"The Englishman returned home Friday evening. To approach him and ask who was coming to the farm and why, or to just wait until Saturday came around, caused a dilemma for me. Fortunately, I didn't have to decide which to do. After supper on Friday, The Englishman shocked me by saying, "Come, son, let's take a walk and talk."

"You can well imagine the look of surprise that spread across my face. First of all, it was the first time in my fifteen years of life that I could recall the Englishman addressing me as 'son.' Secondly, I couldn't imagine what he had to say to me that necessitated our taking a walk.

"Minutes later, we were standing just inside the barn. I was right! The big meeting tomorrow has to do with the Underground Railroad, were my thoughts immediately prior to the Englishman's first words since we left the house.

"George tells me that you asked about the guests we're having tomorrow. But, before I tell you about them, I need to let you in on a few other things. Some of which might surprise you."

That's what you think, I thought as I followed the Englishman to the stall that concealed the hidden room. Before going any further, he swore me to secrecy.

It was difficult for me, but when he showed me the room and explained what it was used for, I acted as if it was all brand new to me. For the next several hours I sat in silence, listening to the Englishman as he told me all about slavery, abolitionists, the mood of the country and his involvement in it all.

It took a lot for me to sit and listen without letting on that I knew lots about abolitionists, and both sides of the slavery question. I strained to refrain from telling the Englishman that I had discovered my mother's trunk in the attic, I had read her scrapbooks, and I had been adding to them for the past few years. I wanted to tell him that I read every newspaper and magazine I got my hands-on that contained an article on slavery and/or the abolitionist's movement. One by one, the Englishman went down the list of expected guests, giving me a brief background description of each.

All the while he spoke, my mind was elsewhere. He wasn't telling me anything I didn't already know. So whenever he named one of the anticipated guests, I tried to imagine what they were like. To read accounts about them and their exploits was one thing, to actually stand face to face with them, was another.

It was rather late when we returned to the house. It had been a long and tiring day, so I went straight to bed. For the longest time, I lay flat on my back staring up at the ceiling. Although I had guessed that the Englishman was involved with the Underground Railroad, I never imagined he was involved as deeply as he was. The list of people who were expected and the fact they were gathering at our house, made me realize the Englishman, my father, was a leading figure in the abolitionist movement.

The fact that I had never read about him did puzzle me at first. After giving it much thought, I concluded that he probably went to great lengths to keep his involvement with the Underground Railroad a secret. After all, he was a wealthy and well-known man in New York. I surmised that, for obvious reasons, he and his tremendous wealth could best serve the cause if his involvement was known only to a select few people. Eventually, I drifted to sleep.

The sound of a carriage pulling up in front of the house woke me. It was pitch dark in my room. I stumbled out of bed and hastily headed for the window to get a glance at whomever had just arrived. On my way to the window, I stumbled over my boots and fell to the floor. By the time I picked myself up, reached the window and peered out, whomever it was had already entered the house. Without wasting another minute, I got dressed and headed downstairs. The Englishman met me at the bottom of the steps and blocked my way.

"Where do you think you're going, It's three in the morning Shouldn't you be asleep?"

"I heard a carriage pull up a few minutes ago and I wanted to see who had arrived."

"Don't worry about that. Go on back to bed. You'll hear carriages arriving throughout the night, but I don't expect to see you again until sometime after the sun comes up. Do I make myself clear?"

"Yes Sir," I responded disappointedly.

"Good night, Joseph."

"Good night, Sir," I turned away and headed back up the steps.

The sound of the rooster crowing woke me the second time. I lay still in bed trying to remember having fallen back asleep.

The early morning light was starting to shine through the window, and there was an almost unreal stillness in the air. My stomach was in knots. The evening before, when I sat listening to the Englishman run down the list of invited guests, I could tell that he hadn't mentioned everyone who was expected. I climbed out of bed, tip-toed over to the door and carefully cracked it open. There wasn't a sound to be heard, so I decided to wait in my room until I was sure that everyone was up and gathered together in the same room.

The next hour and a half seemed to drag on forever. Every ten minutes or so, I heard someone moving about in the hall. You had to pass my door to get to the steps leading downstairs.

"For the past fifteen minutes, there had been no movement outside, so I concluded that everyone had gone downstairs. Anxiously, I got out of bed and put on my boots. When I returned to my room earlier, I hadn't bothered to take my clothes off again. It took me less than five minutes from when I climbed out of bed to reach the bottom of the steps. Voices could be heard coming from the dining room. To say that I was nervous would be sort of an understatement. It took me another five minutes to get up enough courage to enter the dining room. Just as I appeared in the doorway, the Englishman stood up. 'Ah, there you are Joseph. Come in. Let me introduce you to our distinguished guests.' "

It was at that point in Pop's story that I interrupted him. "I bet you I know a lot about everyone who was there, just like you did Pop. I read a book on freedom fighters and abolitionists today," I boasted proudly.

"Well, we'll see about that. Tell you what. As I name each of the guests who were there, you can tell us what you know about them."

"Okay!"

"The first person I was introduced to, was Henry Highland Garnett."

"He was a minister and an outspoken critic of slavery," I responded.

"Good. Then I met Arthur Tappan and Lewis Tappan."

"They were two wealthy white men who supported the antislavery movement."

Pop smiled approvingly, and continued. "Charles B. Ray and George T. Downing were there."

"Businessmen."

"Dr. James McCune Smith was in attendance."

"He was a noted Negro physician," was my quick response.

"Dr. Henry Ward Beecher and Charles L. Reasoner," Pop blurted, hoping to stump me.

"Minister and educator!"

"When I was introduced to Robert Purvis," Pop continued, "I was momentarily confused. He was known to me from my readings and he didn't look at all like I expected. Like myself, he was a product of a white father and a Negro mother. While the Negro in me was dominant, it didn't show in him at all. If he had a mind to, he could have easily passed for white."

"I read about him today also," I cut in. "His father was a successful Charleston merchant and his mother" was a free Negro. His father sent him north where he was educated at Amherst. His father willed him a small fortune and he settled in Philadelphia. He never tried to pass for white. Instead, he proudly let it be known that he was a mulatto, and openly joined the fight against slavery."

"Hum, you know more about him than I knew. The fact that Robert Purvis came all the way from just outside of Philadelphia to attend the meeting, added to the excitement at hand. Then, when I was introduced to the next guest, I froze. I couldn't believe that I was standing in the same room with this great man. He was one of my true heroes. Stories about him abounded in just about every newspaper I read. If there was in fact a leader of Negroes, he was it. Frederick Douglass was just as stately in appearance as I imagined him to be. Like Robert Purvis and myself, his father was also white. Unlike my father and Purvis' father, his father denied him."

Pop paused waiting for me to say something. I didn't bother to say anything about Frederick Douglass because I knew that Pop was aware that I knew all about him. He had told me lots of stories about Douglass.

"Well," Pop continued. "As awed as I was at meeting Mr. Douglass, it didn't come close to how I felt when I was introduced to the next guest. She was the only woman present. Before I even knew who she was, I could sense that she was, without a doubt, a leader of men and a great woman. When I heard her name, I almost fainted. I had read about her, but had never seen a picture of her. Just recently, I read that a $40,000 reward had been offered for her capture. Never, in my wildest dreams, did I imagine that I would ever come face to face with Harriet Tubman. She didn't look at all like I had imagined. Based on stories that I had read about her feats, I expected to see a large muscular woman. She looked kind of frail but when she greeted me, the strength was clear in her voice. Want me to go on or do you want to tell us what you know about Harriet Tubman, Goldie?"

"Come on, Goldie, tell us about her," Sam urged.

"Okay. Harriet Tubman was a leader or conductor in the Underground Railroad movement and made numerous trips into the South to lead slaves to freedom. She safely led more than 300 slaves out of the bonds of slavery to the North and Canada. She was a runaway slave herself. Once she set out along the Underground Railroad with her passengers, no one failed to complete the trip, involuntarily or otherwise. Harriet Tubman made it clear that if anyone wanted to quit along the way or turn back, she would shoot them before she allowed them to quit. She was a firm believer in the old expression, "Dead men tell no tales." Later, during the Civil War, she served as a spy for the Union army."

"Well done, Goldie, well done," Pop congratulated me. Sam and Helen also expressed surprise at my seemingly extensive knowledge about such famous people from the past.

"What happened after you met everyone? What were they meeting about?" I asked.

"When the introductions were completed, I joined them at the table for breakfast. Some of the people gathered hadn't seen each other in years and others were meeting for the first time. Most of the conversation at the table centered around old times and getting to know each other better. Aside from knowing the obvious, that these great people were gathered together to discuss the issue of slavery, I never did get to know any specifics because after breakfast, they retreated to the secret room under the barn floor. Ben and Chester stood guard outside and no one was allowed near the barn. George took them refreshments around noon and they stayed huddled together in the room until after sunset.

"There was a huge feast for supper, after which everyone retired to the parlor and again engaged in general conversation. Around nine p.m., the guests began to depart. Every twenty minutes or so, a carriage was brought around to the front of the house and several guests departed.

It was just past midnight when Harriet Tubman got up to leave. Before she climbed into the waiting carriage, she looked me dead in the eyes and spoke. 'It'll be up to you and future generations to continue what we've started. The struggle for freedom and equality for all Negroes will be a long one. We're fighting for it now. You'll have to continue the fight and prepare your children to do the same.' All the while, Harriet Tubman spoke to me, I stood mesmerized, staring back into her eyes as if I were in a hypnotic trance. When she was through addressing me, Miss Tubman and the Englishman hugged, then bade each other good night. A few minutes later, the carriage carrying this great lady disappeared into the night. Harriet Tubman was the last guest to depart.

After the Englishman and George retired for the night, I quietly made my way back downstairs to the living room. I can't describe to you the feeling that came over me as I looked around the now empty room. Sheer power lingered in the room. Never again in life would I experience that feeling. You would have to stand in a room where so many great people gathered to experience it, Pop concluded.

My thoughts were broken when the mortician tapped me lightly on the shoulder. I jumped from his unexpected touch. "Excuse me Mr. Covington, would you like to take a last look at your grandfather before I close the casket?"

"Yes, I would. Thank you."

The first thing I noticed as I walked toward Pop's casket was that the church was now almost empty.

"Pop," I said, reaching into the casket and taking hold of his hand. I know how you felt that night back on the farm. I feel it now as I stand here. A lot of great people were in here a few minutes ago and they were all here to say good-bye to you because of who you were. You were every bit as great as were your childhood heroes." I leaned over and kissed him goodbye, then called the mortician over to close the casket.

## CHAPTER SEVEN

**B**y the time I exited the church, most of those who had come to pay their last respects to the man they knew as Joseph Cinque Covington, were gone. One of Pop's last requests was that before being laid to rest, he wanted to be driven on a final tour around Harlem and other parts of the city that had been his home.

Because of his unusual request, it was announced during the service that the burial services would not take place immediately following the funeral services. Instead, those who wished to pay further respects to Pop could either gather back in front of the church at one p.m. and join in the funeral procession to the cemetery in Brooklyn, or they could join the mourners again at the burial site at two p.m.

Arrangements had been made for a military escort to accompany the hearse around the city. Arranged by my childhood friend Herby, the escort consisted of several jeeps borrowed from the local armory and manned by Negro veterans of several wars.

Our house had always been like a second home to Herby. Besides Helen, Sam, and myself, Herby was one of the few people who had the privilege of listening to Pop's stories. He was a year and a half older than me and had joined the New York National Guard shortly after his seventeenth birthday.

He claimed that Pop's stories about his service with the Massachusetts Fifty-fourth during the Civil War had inspired him to sign up. Herby wanted to be ready to join in the fight when the United States entered the big war, so he volunteered to become a member of the 15th Regiment of the Guard.

Through the efforts of a Harlem civic organization in which Pop was an active member, the 15th Regiment had just come into existence. The Equity Congress managed to extract a promise from William Sulzer, the Democratic candidate for governor in 1912. If elected, he promised that he would authorize the formation of a Negro Regiment in the state militia. When Sulzer was elected, he kept his promise. In 1913, he signed into law, a bill mandating the establishment of the State's first all Negro National Guard units. However, it wasn't until three years later that the law took effect.

It was under the new Republican governor, Charles Whitman that the order was actually given to form the first Negro Regiment. Despite the fact that it carried no provisions for a headquarters or any equipment, formation of the unit got underway.

Colonel William Hayward, a white National Guard officer who was assigned the task of establishing the unit, encountered little difficulty in attracting recruits. Herby was one of the first who proudly joined up. To tell the truth, had I been old enough, I probably would have enlisted myself. An old abandoned Harlem dance hall served both as headquarters and drill hall for the 15th Regiment. Lacking weapons, the new recruits substituted broom sticks for rifles during their drills.

Despite the obvious lack of support by the leaders of the State Guard, members of the 15th Regiment of the New York National Guard displayed their pride. To the delight of the Negroes in Harlem, they frequently paraded down Fifth Avenue, proudly marching with their broom sticks at shoulders arms. I was standing in a mixed crowd during one such parade, and to this day, I remember how many of the white folks standing around ridiculed them, laughing about the "Negroes playing soldier." They didn't care if any of us who had come to watch the 15th march heard what they said. To them, the entire affair was one big joke.

Even though the Regiment was an official part of the New York National Guard, the Federal Government refused to recognize its validity until the United States joined in World War I. Four months after war was declared by the United States Congress, the 15th was activated and sent to join other units of the New York Guard for training in Spartanburg, South Carolina.

A good number of the recruits in the 15th had never been exposed to the southern way of things. Several racially motivated incidents, which almost turned into riots, occurred both in town and at camp while the Regiment was stationed in South Carolina. The Regiment was transferred back to Long Island, New York, on November 16, 1917, where they were met by white troops from Mississippi and Alabama. On the first night of their arrival, racially sparked fights broke out. The next day, the 15th Regiment was shipped out to join the war in France. They were the first American combat troops to engage the enemy in World War I. Most of what I learned about the Regiment and its exploits in combat, I learned from Herby after he returned from the war.

It was a big moment for him when he told Pop, Sam, and me all about the war in Europe. It had been several weeks after he returned home. We had just finished a dinner in his honor at our house and the four of us had retreated to the living room. Pop insisted that Herby sit in his favorite chair and tell us all about his tour with the "Hell Fighters," the name earned by the 369th Regiment while in Europe. The official designation of the 15th Regiment had been changed to the 369th Regiment. Herby, who had always been a bit of a showman, imitated Pop to a tee. He leaned back in the chair, rubbed his chin and began.

"The story that I'm about to tell you is true, at least as I remember it. I may be getting old, but my memory is still damn good."

Before continuing, Herby stopped and joined us as we laughed at his impersonation of Pop. Then, as if something had suddenly taken possession of him, Herby got a very serious look on his face as he continued.

"As the first troops to reach France, we were immediately thrust into battle. We fought in Belleau Woods, at Chateau Terry, at Vosges, at the Metz and lots of places in between."

We sat for hours, listening while Herby told us about battle after battle that the 369th and the other all Negro units fought. The other units were the 370th, the 371st and the 372nd. He told us about how his unit, the 369th, was the first allied unit to reach the Rhine.

"We were under intense and continuous fire from the Germans for 191 days. They threw everything that they had at us and try as they might, they never took a trench we held, or captured one of our soldiers. We didn't lose a foot of ground to them," he boasted proudly. "For our efforts, our Regiment was awarded the French Croix de Guerre and so was the 371st and the 372nd Regiments. A good number of men in all three Regiments were awarded numerous medals for individual acts of bravery."

Herby's story was full of accounts of heroism. The story that stood out clearest in my mind was one that Herby referred to as "The Battle of Henry Johnson."

"It was early on the morning of May 18, 1918 that The Battle of Henry Johnson took place. I just missed being a part of that battle.

"Originally, I had been assigned to the same observation dugout as Johnson. At the last minute, I was ordered to the rear for a meeting of NCOs. To this day, I don't know if that was a twist of fate for the better or for the worse, because I sure would have liked to have been in the hole with Henry when the Germans attacked.

"Anyway, it was early in the morning when Henry Johnson and his good buddy Needham Roberts heard somebody clipping away at the barbed wire in front of their observation dugout. Several other soldiers in the hole were fast asleep. Johnson immediately set off a few rockets to signal us that the enemy was trying to break through the lines. The Germans responded by showering the observation post with a barrage of grenades that almost destroyed the post while trapping the other men on duty and critically wounding Needham. Johnson wasted no additional time. Without hesitating for another second, he opened fire on the Germans with his rifle.

"Meanwhile, Needham, who had managed to pull himself up against the side of the dugout, hauled grenades at the enemy until he fell from his wounds. When Johnson ran out of bullets he engaged in hand to hand combat with the Germans who were still trying to overrun the post. One of them managed to get into the dugout and capture Roberts, but before the enemy soldier could retreat with his prisoner, Johnson jumped the German and freed his buddy. A few seconds later, one of the Germans who Johnson had knocked out, came to and shot him. Only quick thinking saved Johnson. He dropped to the ground and pretended he was dead. When the German approached to check his body, Johnson rolled over and plunged his bayonet into him. Johnson then sprang back to his feet and began treating the Germans to a dose of American hand grenades, forcing the remainder of the enemy patrol to retreat. One of the men trapped by fallen debris in the dugout estimated the number of retreating Germans to be close to two dozen.

For their heroic actions that morning, Privates Henry Johnson and Needham Roberts, were the first American privates to be awarded the Croix de Guerre, France's highest award for bravery.

"It wasn't just the Germans that we had to contend with over there in France. We had to contend with a lot of racial shit, too."

"Yeah, I read about some of the shit they put you guys through over there."

"Reading about it is one thing, Goldie, living it was another. It wasn't the Frenchies as much as it was our fellow Americans who put us through the bullshit that we had to deal with when we weren't fighting. See, them redneck boys from down South and a good number of them northern, liberal, white boys brought that Jim Crow nonsense overseas with them. They started spreading all kinds of lies about how we were to the French. They told them to hide their women folk from us because they weren't safe around us. Told them that all a 'nigger' wanted out of life was a piece of white ass. Now that's pretty funny considering that most white women ain't got no ass."

We all busted out laughing at Herby's remark but he cut our laughter short and continued talking.

"White officers weren't no better. They openly encouraged French officers to avoid any social contact with Colored officers. We didn't take the Army's racist attitude without letting them know that we were annoyed about it, to say the least. Matter of fact, we went so far as to embarrass the brass one day. I thought about you, Mr. Covington, when we did it. Remember how you organized a pay strike during the Civil War?"

"Sure, do you mean you did the same thing?"

"Not quite. But we let it be known that we weren't pleased about things. On Thanksgiving evening, the Army was having this big ceremony just outside of Metz. They wanted to impress the French, wanted to show them that we were good old American boys and proud of it. They gathered all three thousand of us Colored troops together in a field. There would have been more of us present, but we had suffered over eleven hundred casualties a month earlier while fighting at Champagne. Well anyway, once we were all gathered together, the regimental band began playing and we were told to sing "My Country Tis of Thee." Unknown to the few white officers who were with us, the word had been passed around earlier about what the gathering was for, and none of us planned to sing a word. We stood there in silence as the music drowned out the voices of the white officers who were the only ones singing. We got our message across. What was especially gratifying was that there was this one Colored officer, who was held in the highest regard by all us Colored soldiers and even his white fellow officers, who stood with us in protest. Yes sir, it did us proud to have First Lieutenant Lane join in."

"Way to go!" I exclaimed before adding, "I've kept up with the war as much as I could, but the press sure has done a good job of keeping secret the fact that a lot of Colored soldiers were heroes."

"They did a better job of keeping it a secret that there were Colored officers serving with us as well. Take Lieutenant Lane I just told you about. He was an inspiration to all of the Colored troops. Elisha Lane was his full name. He was from North Carolina. Some of us men got to know him pretty well. There was something about him that just made you proud to know him. I suspect it had a lot to do with his upbringing and the way he carried himself. He didn't seem to be afraid to let it be known that he was Colored and damn proud of it. He came from a prominent family in Wilson, North Carolina. His father was a well-respected African Methodist minister named William Leander Lane, First Lieutenant Lane told us that his father and mother taught him to be proud of who and what he was. He was always there for us Colored troops when we needed someone to talk with. He was right up front in battle too. He was awarded the Croix de Guerre of France for individual bravery and the Purple Heart for wounds suffered in battle. Yeah, we were especially proud of him."

Herby paused long enough to catch his breath, then continued. Every bit of the suffering in battle and all the racism we had to put up over there while fighting, seemed worthwhile when we arrived back on American soil and saw the crowd that was waiting for us. They were cheering as loud as you could imagine. It was especially touching when we reach Harlem.

It was just a few weeks before we had the dinner in Herby's honor that the warriors of the 369th Regiment disembarked from the ships that carried them back home from the war. They were greeted by a million cheering New Yorkers who piled in the streets to watch them parade beneath the Victory Arch in Washington Square Park and up Fifth Avenue. Negroes were mixed in with the crowd of onlookers all along the parade route. I was waiting for them just outside of the park on Seventh Street and Fifth Avenue and I followed their march for more than five miles, all the way to Harlem. When the 369th reached Harlem, you could feel the excitement all around, and it didn't take much looking to see the pride in the faces of the Hell Fighters as they were greeted by more than one hundred thousand cheering Negro citizens of Harlem.

Herby stayed in the National Guard after the war and had risen to the rank of Master Sergeant. Getting permission to use the Guard's vehicles to escort the hearse around was an easy task for him.

"You okay, Goldie?" Once again, I had been lost in my private thoughts. Herby's familiar voice momentarily startled me.

"You okay Goldie?" he repeated.

"Yeah, yeah, I'm fine. I was just reminiscing about that evening you first shared your war time experiences with us. Thanks a lot for arranging the escort. Pop would have liked the idea of a military escort for his final ride around town."

"What do you mean would have liked? Don't you know old soldiers never die. Your grandfather's spirit is sitting in heaven right next to Helen, looking down at this whole thing."

"Well how do you like your escort, Pop?" I whispered while turning my head toward the sky. I fought to hold back the tears. "Damn! I'm going to miss him, Herby."

**Gets Medal**

ELISHA LANE
First lieutenant, retired, Eighth
Regiment Officers Reserve corps,
who has been presented with the
medal of the Order of the Purple
Heart by the United States government. Lieutenant Lane also
holds the Croix de Guerre of France
for his heroism during the war. He
lives at 5440 Indiana Ave.

"We're all gonna miss him, Goldie. But as long as we keep our memories of him alive; it's like he's just gone on another one of his business trips." Herby patted me on my shoulder reassuringly.

"That's true. Pop used to always say that a person lives as long as people remember them."

"He was right you know, and that being the case, Joseph Covington is going to be around a long time. Now let's give them a hand with those flowers so we can get rolling. You know your grandfather was always one for being on time." Herby's light humor was appreciated.

"Thanks Herby."

"For what, man? Come on let's give them a hand."

We reentered the church and proceeded to gather the numerous flowers and wreaths.

"I've never seen so many flowers in one place in all my life. There are more flowers here than in any flower shop I've been in," Herby commented. "I'll pull the cards off them so you'll know who to send thank you notes to."

"I'll give you a hand."

"Can you hold on a second?" Herby called to one of the attendants who was on his way out of the church with a wreath in each hand. "I want to get the cards off the wreaths first."

"Yes, Sir," the attendant replied.

Herby walked over to the attendant and removed the cards from the wreaths. "Man, Pop knew them all," he said as he looked at the two cards.

"Who are they from?"

"One is from a Mary McLeod Bethune and I can't believe who the other one is from."

"Well what does it say?"

"It's signed Marcus M. Garvey. I thought he was still in jail, or dead."

"No. They let him out in December of '27 and deported him back to Jamaica. I sure wish that he could have been here to speak today. Pop would have loved it."

It was true, although Pop didn't agree with a lot of Marcus Garvey's politics, he admired Garvey's abilities as an orator and would have considered it an honor to have him speak at his funeral. Pop used to say that there was a-lot about Marcus Garvey's philosophy to be admired. When Marcus Garvey spoke, whether you agreed with him or not, you listened.

It didn't surprise me that word of Pop's passing had reached Garvey in Jamaica. He still had a few followers in town. If nothing else, Marcus Garvey could be credited with establishing the first large scale organized social movement among New York's Negro population. He preached that there was no hope or justice for the Negro in America. He believed that American Negroes needed their own country.

Garvey had lots of slogans, but the one that was still the most vivid in my mind was one I heard him shout at the conclusion of a sermon one day at Liberty Hall. Liberty Hall could best be described as a large roofed shed located on 138th Street between Seventh and Lenox Avenues. It was estimated that as many as six thousand people could fit under its roof It sure seemed like there were at least that many people present the day I first heard Marcus Garvey shout, Africa for the Africans at home and abroad!"

That's where he and Pop differed. One evening, back in 1920 after a supper at our house, he and Pop got into a discussion about that very slogan. Pop was a firm believer in Negroes insisting on getting their just due right here in

America. "We built this country. We fought and died for it, and we are entitled to our share of the American dream," was Pop's position.

"Well how long do we have to wait before we get our piece of the pie? Our just due is long overdue," Garvey countered. "Besides, what we think is due us and what the white man thinks we're due, are two entirely different things. How many more lynchings have to take place? How many more riots, like the one's last year, have to occur before we're allowed to share in that dream you're talking about? If we stay here in America, equality, opportunity and justice will always be just that for the Negro, a dream."

It was at that point in their discussion that I sort of let my mind wander. Whenever someone mentioned the lynchings that were going on around the country, I became unbelievably angry. All my life, I had been reading about lynching, and seeing pictures of Negroes dangling from the end of ropes while smiling white folks stood around jeering and gaping at them. There had been more than sixty lynchings reported in 1918 and eighty-three recorded in 1919. To white folks, the word "picnic" meant pick out a nigger and lynch him. I always found it interesting how certain words originated.

Of the numerous lynchings that I read about, the one that always sprang into my mind whenever someone brought up the subject of lynching, was one of a negro woman that took place in Valdosta, Georgia in 1918. Grown man that I was, when I read a reporter's account of the lynching in the newspaper, I cried. The reporter wrote, The woman was well into her pregnancy when they hung her from the tree. While she was dangling from the tree and still alive, a man ran up and cut her stomach open with a knife. The premature, but live baby, tumbled from the woman's stomach to the ground and began to cry. The baby's cries were quickly silenced by another man who stepped forward and stomped the baby to death, while the other white folks gathered around and cheered him on. Next, several members of the crowd doused their lynched victim with gasoline and set her body ablaze to the delight of the rest of the mob".

The riots, that Marcus Garvey had referred to, took place the past summer. Everyone was calling it the Red Summer of 1919. Before the summer ended, twenty-six riots had broken out. Washington, D.C., along with cities in Nebraska, Texas, Illinois, Tennessee and Arkansas were the scenes of the largest of the riots. There were more than five hundred people injured during the Chicago riot alone.

"We'll never agree on what should be done. But I agree with you whole-heartedly when you say we need to promote and honor our own heroes," was the next thing that I remember hearing Pop say to Marcus Garvey.

"What you thinking about, Goldie?"

I didn't realize that once again I was lost in thought. "Oh, I was just thinking about Garvey."

"That man was something Wasn't he."

"He sure was Herby. He sure was."

Indeed he was. During his tenure in America, Marcus Garvey, founded his own church, the African Orthodox Church. Along with W. A. H. Domingo, William H. Ferris, and Hubert Harrison, he organized and subsequently incorporated the Universal Negro Improvement Association in the United States. Under the umbrella of the U.N.I.A., he set up some of the first cooperatives in Harlem, opened several manufacturing factories and founded a commercial steamship company. It was the steamship company and Back to Africa Movement that landed Garvey on the government's investigative list.

One of the stated goals of the Universal Negro Improvement Association was to Relieve Africa of Anglo-Saxon oppression and domination." Somehow, Garvey should have been more aware that you couldn't go around preaching about kicking the white man out of Africa during the height of his colonization days and not be made to suffer the white man's wrath. He was labeled a threat to the system and the government set out to get him. In 1925, Garvey was arrested and charged with mail fraud. He was convicted on the charges and sent to a Federal prison in Atlanta, Georgia. Two years later he was released from prison and deported to his native Jamaica.

"You never met Mary McLeod Bethune, did you Herby?" I asked while he removed the remaining cards from the sympathy wreaths and other floral arrangements.

"No I haven't, but from what you've told me about her, I would consider it an honor, if I ever do."

It was during a fund raising lecture in New York, while Herby was in France, that I had the privilege of meeting the great Mary McLeod Bethune-Cookman. To this day, I remember how astonished I was when she spoke of how she founded Bethune-Cookman College on a dump site in Daytona, Florida, in 1904. She started out with six black students and a total of $1.50 in cash, and with little more than will power and determination, Mary McLeod Bethune built a college.

Herby handed me the cards he had gathered and we headed out of the church. On the way, I sorted through the cards. There was one from the Lewis family. Although Butch and I wrote each other frequently, I hadn't seen him or his family for a good number of years.

Mr. Lewis moved his family to an all-Negro town named Boley in Oklahoma, back in 1913. He figured there was a lot of money to be made by an enterprising Colored man in an all Negro town. He did make a lot. In fact he struck it rich. The year after he arrived in Oklahoma, Ed Lewis began speculating in land in Boley and Langston. Langston was north of Boley and had been the first all-Negro town established back in 1891, when the state was still a territory.

Pop used to always say that Ed Lewis was followed around by a cloud of luck. In 1914, shortly after he arrived in Oklahoma, Mr. Lewis began buying up as much land as he could get his hands on. As long as he could get the mineral rights along with the soil rights and the price of the land was right, he bought it. He obtained most of his land from other Negroes who left to return to Africa with Alfred Sam Charles, an adventurer who wanted to start a colony of American Negroes in Africa. Next thing anyone knew, Ed Lewis and his family were in the oil business.

By the time I reached the limousine and climbed inside, I had quickly glanced at most of the cards Herby and I had collected. On my way into the limousine, I was putting the cards in my inside jacket pocket for safekeeping, when one of them fell to the ground. I leaned over the side of the limo and picked it up. My eyes scanned the card as I put it into my pocket with the rest. The message was all too familiar, "With heartfelt sympathy," but the name on the card surprised me.

"A'Leillia Robinson, now who would have thought that she would remember Pop?" On that thought, I slid back in the limo seat.

A minute later, Sam climbed into the limousine and sat next to me. He had been busy with a few last minute details. Sam was all the family I had left, now that Pop and Helen were gone.

"Are you okay, Goldie?" he inquired.

"I'm fine. I was just sitting here trying to figure out how A'Leillia Robinson remembered Pop. She sent a huge wreath to the church."

"Did she sign the card A'Leilla Robinson?"

"Yep."

"That's unusual, she almost always signs her name A'Leillia Walker Robinson. She sure is proud of her family name, as well she should be. Do you remember her mother, Madame C.J. Walker?"

"How could anyone forget her?"

"Not easily, Goldie, not easily."

"Remember all the commotion she caused when she built her mansion around the corner from you, Sam?"

"Do I remember? Sure I do. It's one of the places Joseph wanted us to ride past. Boy, did that gal have style."

"Indeed she did!"

While I waited for the procession to get underway, I thought about Madame C.J. Walker. As far as Pop was concerned, she was a female Horatio Alger.

In 1913, Pop bought a brownstone on 139th Street between Seventh and Eighth Avenues. The purchase was made possible only because Pop was heavily involved in real estate. Most of his holdings were located downtown near the Village and in the midtown area. He struck up a deal with a white realtor who desperately wanted to acquire several lots that Pop owned on Forty-fourth Street. Pop agreed to sell the realtor the property only after he agreed to sell Pop a house he owned on Strivers Row that he had recently put up for sale.

At first, I wasn't very pleased about moving further uptown, especially to Strivers Row because there were too many white folks still living there. Most of my childhood experiences with white people hadn't been too pleasant. But since I was still a minor and under Pop's care, I didn't have much choice in the matter.

It didn't take me long to get used to my new surroundings. One hundred and Thirty-ninth Street, between Seventh and Eighth Avenues, was a picturesque street. The entire block was lined with trees and always immaculately clean.

The best thing about moving further uptown was that our new home had a carriage house out back which had been converted into a garage. Pop didn't believe in letting things go to waste, so he finally bought an automobile. He didn't drive it much. Most of the mileage that had been logged on the car, before Pop gave it to me on my eighteenth birthday, had accumulated from Sam's use of it.

Another good thing about moving to 139th Street was that we were once again living near Sam. A year earlier he had purchased a brownstone over on One-hundred-thirty-fifth Street, just off Seventh Avenue.

John Covington, Pop's father, whom he never stopped referring to as the Englishman, sold the farm out on Long Island while Pop was off fighting in the Civil War. Less than three months after Pop mustered out of the Army, the Englishman passed away, leaving Pop a fortune in cash, gold and real estate. By the time I was born, Pop had turned the fortune over several times. He was involved in several joint real estate ventures in Harlem with other Negro realtors. Most of the ventures had gone sour, but Pop managed to get out before they went bust.

Pop had interests in the company that sold Madame C.J. Walker three lots and brownstones on 136th Street. It was when the brownstones were torn down and they began building her ninety thousand dollars plus, Indiana limestone house, later known as "The Castle," that people began to talk about the mysterious woman from St. Louis or Denver.

It wasn't until after Madame C.J. Walker moved to town that the full story of how she accumulated her wealth became known. Madame C.J. Walker was working as a laundress in St. Louis when she figured out a way of straightening hair, or as she once put it once during dinner at our house, "One day when I was stealing a nap, I had a dream that showed me a method of banishing the stubborn, lusterless crinkle from Negro hair, transforming it into shining smoothness." It must have been one dandy of a dream because in less than ten years, she had transformed it into a multi-million dollar enterprise. Her hair care manufacturing plant produced products that became household words in many Negro homes throughout the United States and in at least two dozen foreign countries.

Aside from the fact that she was a successful business person and nice in general, Pop had a fondness for Madame Walker because, like himself, she enjoyed entertaining Unlike

Pop, she chose her guests more along social lines. Her parties were lavish affairs attended by affluent and influential Negroes from all over the country. Yet, all the influential people she knew couldn't help her surmount the objections of white folks in Flushing, Long Island in 1916 when Madame Walker attempted to purchase some property on which to build a country home in the Bishop Court section of the neighborhood.

After a bitter fight, Madame Walker ended up building her country home at Irvington-on-the-Hudson, one of the most exclusive areas in New York State in 1917. She commissioned the Negro architect, Vertner W. Tandy to design her Georgian stucco mansion.

Unfortunately, she didn't enjoy her home for the many years that she looked forward to spending there. Madame Walker passed away late in the spring of 1919.

Madame Walker willed large sums of money to various Negro charities, including one hundred thousand dollars to an academy for girls in West Africa that she had founded several years earlier. The bulk of her estate, which was estimated to be in the two million dollar range, was left to her only daughter, A'Leillia.

During the past few years, I had devoted most of my leisure time to trying to earn a living as a writer. Generally, I wasn't that socially active. As a result, I lost contact with a good number of people. A'Leillia was one of them.

On the other hand, Pop was still active in his many business ventures right up until he had his stroke. I used to spend several days a week with him learning about his businesses. He was preparing me to one day take over where he left off. Still, he knew that my interests were with writing and encouraged me in my pursuit of a career as a novelist. He used to say, "You can always hire someone to look after your day-to-day business affairs, but you'll have to occasionally look over their shoulders. When you do, you'll need to know what you're looking at."

The last time I had seen A'Leillia was at her wedding back in 1923. It was some wedding. She called it the "Million Dollar Wedding." It was held at St. Philips and during the ceremony, close to ten thousand people milled around outside trying to get a peak inside the church. By her own estimates, A'Leillia claimed to have spent more than sixty thousand dollars on the wedding.

"I didn't know that Pop was friendly with Madame Walker's daughter."

My sudden comment startled Sam, who had apparently been lost in his own thoughts.

"You say something Goldie?"

"Yeah, I said, I didn't know that A'Leilla Walker was in touch with Pop."

"She wasn't. She's a client of mine. But she remembers Joseph from the good old days. Apparently, she also remembers how highly her mother used to speak of him, and I guess she just wanted to say good-bye for her mother."

"That was nice of her. Maybe Pop and his old friend, Madame Walker, are once again visiting with each other, wherever they are," I commented as the limousine began to move.

**B**efore the funeral service began, I had given the driver of the military jeep leading the procession a list of the places that Pop wanted to pass for the last time. The actual route that would be taken was left to the driver's discretion.

After departing from Saint Philip's Church, the procession proceeded east on 134th Street to Lenox Avenue where it made a right turn, rolled along for another block, then turned right again into 133rd Street. As we proceeded, I gazed out the limousine window at the many clubs that lined the block. The street was called Beale Street by the residents of Harlem. Most of the clubs located on 133rd Street between Lenox and Seventh Avenues catered to the white tourists who came to Harlem to savor the famous night life. They patronized Pod & Jerry's, the Madhouse, the Nest, Catagonia's, Mexico's, and other clubs on the block. One of the most popular clubs on Beale Street was Gladys Bentley's Clam house. Pop took me there on my twenty-first birthday. The differences in the decor between Bentley's and the clubs in Harlem that most Negroes frequented were unbelievable.

Following our brief stop in front of Pod and Jerry's we proceeded west along 133rd Street until we reached Public School 119. The driver of the jeep leading the procession stopped a few feet past the school in order to allow the hearse to stop directly in front of the building.

Public School 119 was important to Pop. He had fought one of his biggest battles with the city over the school's curriculum. The school's administration, sanctioned by the Board of Education, took pride in announcing that it trained Negroes for suitable jobs. What that meant in plain English was that the school's curriculum centered around courses in cooking and sewing. Almost right up until the day he died, Pop was fighting with the Board of Education, trying to get them to add more academic subjects to the school's curriculum.

"It's bad business to teach young people that the only jobs they're suitable to fill are those in kitchens, laundries, and the numerous factories of the garment district. That's why so many of our people are locked into certain job categories."

What Pop said about so many Harlem residents being locked into certain job categories was true. Although there were Negroes living in Harlem who were engaged in just about every professional service that was offered in the city, the vast majority of the Negro men in Harlem were employed in a limited number of professions. They worked as porters, janitors, teamsters, elevator operators, chauffeurs, waiters, and a variety of other unskilled manual labor fields.

By the late twenties, most of the Negro women in Harlem and the few that lived elsewhere, worked as domestics, in laundries or the sweatshops of New York's thriving garment industry.

"Has the Board of Education done anything to change the curriculum at the school, yet?" I inquired of Sam.

"Not really. As usual, they made a lot of promises on paper. But as far as I know, there hasn't been any real progress, yet. You can rest assured though, the changes will come. In short order, too."

Although it was a sad occasion, in many ways I was enjoying Pop's final ride around Harlem. Since I was a lifelong resident of Harlem, I had been a witness to the incredible and profound changes that had taken place in the past ten years. It had been years since I took a leisurely walk around Harlem. After I returned from college in Virginia, Pops and I used to take long strolls around Harlem. He was quite fond of pointing out the multitude of speakeasies that were everywhere. They were thinly disguised as sweet shops, drug stores and delicatessens. Everyone knew where they were, even the cops on the beat.

The "darkening" of Harlem was how Pop referred to the mass exodus of white folks and the migration of Negroes into Harlem that occurred while I was away at college. During our frequent walks, Pop and I used to wager on what year the last group of white holdouts would flee from a particular block.

"I'll give it ten years tops and we'll be living from here clear up to 145th Street," Pop said to me one Sunday afternoon as we strolled along 110th Street, the northern border of Central Park and southern border of Harlem.

"Nah, it'll take longer than that. Funny isn't it, Negroes are moving uptown and white folks are moving downtown into our old neighborhoods."

"Lots of things about living in America are funny, Goldie. Some of the things that go on in America can't be anything but funny; and I don't mean funny in a ha ha sense."

"Amen to that!"

Pop's final tour was bringing back some fond memories. When the procession turned down St. Nickolas Avenue, I looked to the left and saw a familiar building. A good friend of mine, named Roscoe, lived there. Roscoe and Margie, his old lady held a rent party at least once a month. The parties weren't really given to raise their rent money. They just liked calling them rent parties. Lots of other folks were having real ones to help pay the inflated rents that white landlords charged their Negro tenants. It was ironic. Just a few years earlier, Negroes couldn't rent an apartment in the very same buildings if their lives depended on it.

Roscoe and Margie's parties were great. There was usually a piano player accompanied by a singer or two, plenty of good southern cooking, and lots of bootleg liquor on hand.

After making a left turn onto 132nd Street, we proceeded east to Seventh Avenue where we turned right. We came to a halt in front of the Lafayette Theatre, situated in the middle of the block between 132nd and 131st Streets. The Lafayette was considered to be America's leading Negro theatre. It was only sixteen years earlier that the theatre abandoned its segregation policies. Prior to 1913, whenever Pop took me to the Lafayette to see some of the leading Negro entertainers perform, we had to sit in the balcony. Back then, restricting Negroes to the balcony was a strictly enforced policy. We didn't linger long in front of the theatre before continuing south along Seventh Avenue.

"Look at all these storefront churches. Seems like for every speakeasy or whorehouse that operates in Harlem, there's a church to accommodate the sinners on Sunday morning when they finish indulging in their favorite vices on Saturday night."

"You're right about that," I remarked in response to Sam's comment.

There were several storefront churches on almost every block we passed along Seventh Avenue. When we reached 126th Street, we had to make an unscheduled stop. There was a traffic accident in the middle of the intersection of 125th Street. A police officer was standing in the intersection, trying to keep the traffic flowing smoothly. While we waited, Sam pointed to a variety store on the northeast corner.

"It's interesting how all this Christian religion abounds in Harlem and yet that store is without a doubt, one of the most prosperous Negro-owned businesses in town."

It was indeed an interesting store. From the outside it looked like any one of the number of variety stores scattered throughout the community. However, once inside, you noticed several differences between that particular store and most of the other variety stores in Harlem. The first thing you noticed was that the owner was a Negro and so were his two employees. The second thing you noticed was that the store stocked a strange product line. The shelves were packed with a variety of so-called medical concoctions. You could purchase Professor Ajapa's herb juice which was guaranteed to cure rheumatism and a long list of other ailments. If a person wanted to get hold of love charms, blessed handkerchiefs, or any number of roots, they could be found there.

Once a friend of mine, who was concerned that his wife was running around on him at night while he was at work, told me that he bought a powder there that was guaranteed to keep a man's wife home at night. He claimed it worked. He swore that once he began mixing it in his wife's tea, she stopped running around on him. Actually, as far as I knew, my friend's wife was absolutely faithful to him and wasn't running around to begin with.

"Do you think any of that stuff they sell in there really works, Sam?"

"I wouldn't swear by it myself because I haven't ever tried any of those concoctions. But I know quite a few people, many of whom I have a great deal of respect for, who will swear on a stack of bibles ten feet high that a few of those powders and roots work damn well."

It didn't take the police long to clear the two automobiles involved in the accident from the intersection and get traffic flowing again. In less than five minutes after it had come to a halt, traffic was once again moving at its regular pace along Seventh Avenue. When the procession reached 125th Street, we turned west. I knew we wouldn't be stopping on 125th Street, we would just ride by a few of the places that Pop requested he be driven past. A lot of the organizations he used to be active in had headquarters above the stores that lined Harlem's main thoroughfare.

125th Street was the center of activity in Harlem. It was the main commercial strip. There were a variety of stores, restaurants, office buildings and several movie houses stretched across 125th Street between Fifth and St. Nickolas Avenues. The busiest section of the strip was between Seventh and Eighth Avenues. Most of the businesses on 125th Street were white-owned and for the most part, white-operated. That wasn't out of the ordinary, considering a good seventy percent of Harlem's business establishments were white owned and operated.

What was disturbing was that a good number of the stores on 125th Street blatantly practiced discrimination in their hiring practices. Most of the white owned businesses in Harlem were small family-owned stores with two or three employees. It could be understood why they didn't employ many Negroes. Since they were family-operated, they generally employed members of their immediate family to fill the few jobs they generated.

That wasn't the case with some of the other stores on 125th Street. They were much larger and the vast majority of the employees of these establishments were not related to the owners of the business concerns. The only thing that the people who worked in these businesses had in common with their employers was that they were white. The few businesses that employed local residents, employed them as janitors, cooks and elevator operators. For years, Pop and other civic leaders had been waging a battle against the two larger stores on the strip to alter their employment practices. Pop felt that if the larger businesses set an example by hiring local residents, the others would soon follow suit.

One of the stores they were pressuring into changing its hiring practices was Kress' Five and Ten Cents Store. Opened in 1920, Kress' was housed in the building that was once the home of the famous Paspt Restaurant. Kress eventually yield to community pressure and added a few Negroes to its janitorial and stock room staff.

"Has Blumsteins hired anyone from the community, yet?" I inquired of Sam as we passed Blumstein's Department Store, located a few doors down from Kress.

"Not yet, and from what I can tell, they have no intention of hiring any of us anytime soon, at least not voluntarily. When Blumsteins first opened back in 1896 and for a few years afterward, they didn't appreciate any Colored folks coming through the store doors for any reason. Now old man L.A. Blumstein is getting richer by the minute off the money Colored folks spend on his overpriced goods. Still, he isn't about to add any color to his lily-white staff. The saddest part is, the man left Germany to get away from the prejudices inflicted on Jews like himself. Now he practices some of those same prejudices against Negroes in their own land. Joseph and I, along with the NAACP and the Urban League have been trying for years to organize a boycott of the damn place, but folks just don't seem to want to go along with it.

After turning off 125th Street, the procession headed south along Eighth Avenue. Pop's passing would leave a void in our lives. Sam and I both knew and understood that. We rode in silence, Sam lost in his thoughts and I in mine.

My thoughts centered around Pop and his lifelong struggles. During the last two decades of his life, Pop had invested a great deal of energy in trying to knock down the barricades of racism that prevented Negroes from having complete access to businesses, housing, recreational and other facilities in the Harlem community and throughout New York City. He was an unsung local hero. Like his father, Pop tried to keep a low profile. He felt that he could best help the Negro cause by using his wealth to fund those organizations and individuals who were in the forefront of the struggle. He gave generously of himself and his money and never sought any recognition or reward for himself.

Pop's monetary contributions were always made anonymously through Sam. Just about everyone who benefited from Pop's commitment to the advancement of the Negro's strive toward full equality, knew that he was the anonymous donor behind much of the funds they received. They respected his obvious wish for anonymity and pretended that they had no idea who their benevolent benefactor was. The number of prominent people who attended Pop's funeral service earlier were evidence of their respect for him.

"Look at that sign. A living testament that your grandfather's struggles weren't all in vain."

My eyes were shut while I reminisced. I must have really been involved with my thoughts because I hadn't even realized that we had turned onto 116th Street and come to a stop in front of Graham Court. The battle to integrate Graham Court was one of the community struggles in which Pop had taken a frontline, active part. When it came to real estate and housing in Harlem, it struck Pop close to home.

Graham Court was a one block long apartment building. It had eight spacious elevators to service the tenants and all the apartments were large, seven to ten room units. The owners of the building owned several other properties in Harlem that were no more than run down slum dwellings which they gladly rented to Negro tenants at inflated prices. On the other hand, they refused to rent apartments in Graham Court to any Negroes no matter who they were or how much money they had. It was the rapid darkening of Harlem and the continued fight of whites to below 110th Street that ultimately led to the opening of Graham Court to Negroes. Still, it was a victory of sorts for Pop, because the owners once swore that they would never rent apartments in Graham Court to Negroes, no matter what. They once stated that they would burn the place down first.

The ride from Graham Court to 150th Street took a good fifteen minutes. Sam and I exchanged stories about Pop along the way. We talked about what a gifted oral historian he was. Sam threw a strong hint at me during our conversation.

"It sure would be a lasting tribute to Joseph if someone would write his biography one day and include a few of his stories in it."

"By some slight chance, you wouldn't be suggesting that I be that someone?"

"Oh, no. You know me, Goldie. I ain't never been one to make suggestions to a person about what they should or shouldn't do with their time. I was merely stating that your grandfather's life would make a pretty interesting book. Of course, it'll take a good writer to do Joseph justice. Maybe the next time I run into James Weldon Johnson, Langston Hughes, Countee Cullen, George Schuyler or Jessie Fauset, I'll suggest it to one of them. I could provide them with all the details they would need to write Joseph's biography."

Sam smiled and waited for my reaction. He knew that I aspired to one day hear my name mentioned in the same breath with the likes of such talented Negro writers.

When he didn't get a response, he continued. "I could ask Jean Toomer, Charles Johnson, or Zora Neale Hurston to write it. Better yet, maybe I'll give Carl Van Vechten a call."

Sam knew that his reference to Van Vechten would get a reaction from me. I'm sure Van Vechten would be the right writer for the job. Maybe he'll give a balanced account of Pop's life, just like the account of life in Harlem he gave in his book," I replied sarcastically.

"Well, the man does have his following. He's made a small fortune off his book. It's already been translated into Russian, Swedish, French, and Japanese. Now the whole world knows what life is 'really' like in Harlem."

After a long pause, Sam rested his head on the seat back, cracked a wry smile, and replied, "That's not a bad idea, Goldie."

During the past several years, white folks had become extremely interested in learning about Harlem. Rumors were abundant about the exotic and thrilling night life that was to be found there. Hordes of white folks descended on Harlem nightly to experience the thrills they had heard about. The only problem was that the side of Harlem the white folks who came uptown were exposed to, was vastly different from the Harlem the residents knew. Most of the owners of the clubs that catered to these white tourists and thrill-seekers barred Negroes from their establishments, unless they were there as part of the entertainment.

A few white folks took it upon themselves to promote Harlem and its night life. Carl Van Vechten was one of them. His novel, the one Sam had referred to, was titled Nigger Heaven. Published in 1926, it became an instant best-seller.

When I read the book, I was angered and offended by it. Van Vechten devoted a good part of his novel to drug use, wanton sex, and other sensationalisms. He even tried to make a few social commentaries in his novel which, in my opinion, were way off base. Still, those who lived outside Harlem and had never been there, and those who only came to socialize at night, took his book to heart and believed that life in Harlem was as Carl Van Vechten described it. "If Pop's story is ever going to be written, then I'll be the one to write it," I promised myself aloud.

The procession rolled ever so slowly past 150th Street, turned onto 151st Street, then turned left at the corner and continued to proceed down Eighth Avenue before turning left again onto 150th Street. When the procession reached Seventh Avenue, the line of cars stopped. We had just driven around the Dunbar Apartment Complex. Pop was instrumental in helping to get the complex built. Back in 1925, Pop, James H. Hubert who was the director of the New York Urban League, and several other community leaders met with John D. Rockefeller, Jr. and asked him for his financial support in helping to build a model housing complex in Harlem for Negro families. Rockefeller agreed to finance the building of the proposed model housing complex.

When completed, Rockefeller's Dunbar Apartments were indeed a model. The large complex, which was a neighborhood within a neighborhood, centered around six apartment houses spread out over five acres. The majority of the more than 500 apartments in the complex contained two to five rooms. The grounds were landscaped with several parks, playgrounds, and gardens. There was even a well-equipped and professionally staffed nursery on the grounds.

Pop was especially pleased when Rockefeller opened the Dunbar National Bank on the grounds to encourage the Negro tenants to save for their future.

"Now is that progress or is that progress?" Sam asked rhetorically just as the limo lurched forward again.

From the Dunbar apartments, the procession headed south on Seventh Avenue until we reached 143rd Street where we turned left. The next stop we made was at the corner of 143rd Street and Lenox Avenue in front of the Cotton Club. The Cotton Club was Harlem's premier night club. The only problem as Pop saw it, was the club's policy of banning most Negroes from it, unless they were part of the nightly entertainment or a member of the famous chorus line.

The Cotton Club's chorus line was made up of what folks called "high yeller gals" and a few white women who passed themselves off as light skinned Negroes.

That was one of the few things about the Cotton Club that amused Pop.

"Never thought I'd live to see the day that white folks would be trying to pass for Colored," he commented to me one day while we walked past the club.

The Negro entertainers who performed there were among the most talented performing artists in the world. White folks came from all around the country to hear and watch them. When Duke Ellington and his band or Cab Calloway and his orchestra appeared at the Cotton Club, there wasn't an empty seat in the house.

Local youths played a game centered around the Cotton Club. They hung out across the street at night and tried to identify as many people entering the club as possible. Whenever a youth correctly identified one of the patrons, they scored points. Politicians were worth one point and gangsters were worth the most, five points.

The next stop we made was at the Abyssinian Baptist Church on 138th Street between Seventh and Eighth Avenues. It was one of two places that I specifically requested the leader of the procession to stop at for a few minutes. Pop was friends with the church's founder and pastor, the Reverend Adam Clayton Powell, Sr. Although I was friends with Adam Clayton Powell, Jr., I hadn't seen the Reverend Powell, Sr. since the church's cornerstone-laying ceremony back in 1923. When we reached the church, the Reverend Powell, who had expected us, was waiting in front. Sam and I climbed out of the limousine and walked toward the back of the hearse where the Reverend met us. He and Sam shook hands and exchanged greetings, then he turned to me and spoke. "Your grandfather was a good man. We will all miss him, Goldie. If there is anything I can do to help you in your grief, feel free to call on me. Adam regrets that he couldn't attend the services. He asked me to extend his sympathy at your grandfather's passing. He'll be home in a couple of weeks and requested that I let you know that he'll see you then."

"Thanks, Reverend Powell."

After our brief verbal exchange, the attendant opened the rear door of the hearse at the Reverend's request. We bowed our head as the Reverend said a few prayers for Pop. Ten minutes later, after we bade the Reverend Adam Clayton Powell, Sr. good-bye, we climbed back into the limousine and were on our way again.

There was one other place we were scheduled to pass on the list I had given the leader of the procession. On the way to the last stop, I caught site of the Gem Theatre as we drove past 136th. It brought back many fond memories. I couldn't remember the number of shows Pop and I had attended there.

It didn't take us long to reach Ed Smalls Sugar Cane Club at 135th Street and Fifth Avenue. I figured the club would be the most fitting last stop along our route because it was without a doubt, Pop's favorite jump joint. Smalls was where Pop used to go when he wanted to let loose. Up until his stroke, Pop was the picture of health. People who met him at the club were always surprised when they found out his age. His answer to them when they asked how he stayed so young looking was, "You know what they say, black don't crack."

The club was also my favorite hangout spot. To get into it you had to descend a steep flight of steps. It was always dimly lit inside. The dance floor, in the center of the club, was surrounded by a bunch of small, round tables.

The club also served as an unofficial meeting place for a lot of the civic organizations that Pop was involved with. Its doors were always open during the day to community groups who needed a place to hold meetings.

At night, Ed Smalls Sugar Cane Club seemed to come to life when people from the community, looking to cut loose and forget their troubles, packed inside.

It was there I learned to do the "mess around" and the "bump." two of the more popular dances in Harlem.

The club was open when we reached it, so I went inside. I wanted to get a souvenir to place inside Pop's casket. I looked around for something suitable and settled on a book of matches with the club's name imprinted on it. It seemed sort of silly, but I felt that Pop would appreciate it. After all, as Herby pointed out, he was somewhere looking down at us.

As I stood in the silence of the club reminiscing, the manager poured a couple of drinks. He handed me one and then proposed a toast: "To Joseph Cinque Covington, may he live on in the memories of those he loved and those who loved him." We tapped glasses, swallowed the liquor and bade each other goodbye.

After I departed Smalls, I went to the back of the hearse, inched open the lid to Pop's casket, placed the book of matches in and closed the casket. A few minutes later, we continued on our way back to Saint Philips.

It was exactly two p.m. when we arrived at the church. Mourners, waiting to join the procession, sat inside the multitude of cars that lined both sides of the street and stretched around the corner for several blocks.

I exited the limousine and thanked Herby for providing the military escort, which wouldn't take part in the procession to the cemetery. I asked him to thank everyone for me and invited him to ride in the limousine with Sam and me to the cemetery.

Before climbing back into the limousine, I took notice of the church's design. The church was English Gothic in style. Pop had been a member of Saint Philip's congregation since the old days, when it was still located downtown. He was proud of the fact that the new church had been designed and built by two Negro architects. I continued to survey the church for a few minutes before I reentered the limo.

By two-fifteen, the long row of automobiles filled with the many people who had come to pay their last respects to Joseph Cinque Covington, was headed downtown toward the Brooklyn Bridge.

## CHAPTER NINE

The cool, crisp spring air flowed through the partially opened limousine window as we continued down Fifth Avenue. From the right window, I could see Central Park and its many trees. The branches swayed gently in the breeze as if they were slow dancing to the beat of a soft melody. It was a bright, sunny day and the afternoon sun's rays radiated between the trees, forming lines of light that gently touched down onto the lush green grass. The grass and trees seemed much greener than they usually were this time of the year. The sounds of children at play could be heard coming from inside the park. I watched as a small flock of birds darted from tree to tree, and squirrels scampered about on the ground. Looking up at the blue skies, I watched several kites that were floating high above the treetops.

And life goes on, I thought momentarily to myself before Sam broke the silence in the limousine.

"The city is changing. Getting too big for me. Maybe I'll retire this year and move to the country. Used to be a lot of open places like Central Park in Harlem when Joseph and I first moved uptown."

"There were still plenty of wooded areas when we were younger," Herby added. "Remember how we used to sneak off to the woods over on St. Nickolas Avenue after school and fight with the Irish boys from- up the hill?"

"I sure do. But those fights weren't nothing compared with the ones we use to have with the Russian and Jewish boys down by Morningside Park."

"Well listen to the two of you. You're damn lucky your grandfather never got wind of how you spent your afternoons. He'd have skinned you alive."

Herby and I smiled at Sam's remark and turned our heads in opposite directions.

Had Pop found out that I was hanging out where I shouldn't have been, I doubted if he would have skinned me alive. Pop never once laid a hand on me. Whenever I did something wrong, he had a way of lecturing me that made it quite clear that I had done something he didn't approve of and that I better not ever do it again. His stern lectures were usually followed by some form of punishment. The punishments Pop dished out were never harsh, unfair or unbearable. Depending on the gravity of my offense, I was either assigned extra chores around the house or grounded for a week or two.

"Yep, things are sure changing," Sam repeated just as we passed the Southern border of Central Park at Fifty-ninth Street.

It was true; a building boom of unprecedented proportions had taken place in mid-Manhattan since the war. Building after building was being constructed. From the looks of things, it seemed that every new builder who came along was trying to build his a little taller than the one next to it. While scanning the many relatively recent additions to the New York City skyline and the additional buildings that were in various stages of construction, I couldn't help comparing what was going on in midtown to what was occurring in Harlem.

"There's a lot of building going on in Harlem, only most of it is inside of already existing buildings."

"It's criminal, too. But what are folks going to do? There simply isn't enough housing to go around in Harlem and landlords are certainly taking advantage of that," Sam commented in response to my statement.

While new buildings were springing up all over Manhattan south of 110th Street, in Harlem most of the work was reconstruction. The vast majority of Harlem's housing stock was owned by white landlords. After their white tenants fled Harlem and the landlords were forced to rent to Negroes, they began converting once spacious apartments into small one to three room units. Brownstones, which used to house a single white family, now served as home to as many as a dozen Negro families. Generally, each floor of these three-story dwellings was divided into studios and one-bedroom apartments. More often than not, several families shared a common bathroom on one floor. In many cases, one or two bathrooms served all three floors.

While I continued to survey the area, my thoughts wandered back to a conversation I had with Pop several weeks earlier. It was on a Saturday morning. Pop invited me over for breakfast. When I arrived and entered the house, things were just as I expected. The aroma from slightly over-fried bacon filled the air and the lingering smell of burning grease was evident.

"That you, Goldie?" Pop shouted from the kitchen.

"It's me, Pop," I answered.

"Breakfast is ready and waiting. I cooked everything just the way I always have."

After Helen passed away, Pop decided against hiring any new live-in help. A combination maid and cook came to the house during the week. On weekends, Pop was left to fend for himself. That wasn't a problem for him because he still loved messing around in the kitchen. I felt sorry for the maid, though, because there was always a mess waiting for her on Monday mornings.

During breakfast, Pop and I laughed and talked about old times. Afterward, Pop poured himself another cup of coffee and suggested that we go in the living room and talk. I stood up and began gathering the dishes from the table. He reached out and rested his hand on mine.

"It's okay, leave the dishes, I'll get them later."

"Alright, Pop, anything you say." While I addressed him, I looked into his eyes. There was something troubling him.

"Are you okay, Pop?"

"I'm fine. Why do you ask?"

"Oh, no reason. No reason at all. Come on, let's go in the living room."

It wasn't long after we were seated that Pop got a very serious look on his face. He let out a long stream of smoke from the cigar he had been puffing.

"I'm proud of the way you turned out, Goldie. You're a good person and a good writer."

"Why thanks, Pop."

"No need to thank me. Just continue to pursue your writing career and doing the other things that make you happy. Lord knows I spent most of my life doing the things that made me happy. You know what brought me the greatest joy in my life?" Pop didn't wait for an answer before he continued. "The greatest joy in my life came from having you around. You kept me young and always reminded me that things were one day going to get better for our people. Me, I won't be around much longer."

"What are you talking about.?" I interrupted.

"Meant what I said. Hell, I'm pushing ninety. How long do you expect me to be around?"

"At least until you're a hundred," I replied lightheartedly.

"Don't want to live that long. I've lived a full life. Had more than most folks, and definitely seen more things than most folks need to see in one lifetime. I don't want to be around to see the misery that's just around the corner."

"What are you talking about now?"

"The signs are everywhere. Anybody who knows a little about economics ought to be able to see the writing on the wall. Things can't keep on going like they are. What goes up, eventually must come back down. Things are going to go bust. Sold all my stocks the other day, except for my AT&T stock. If you know what's good for you, you'll do the same. You know, I've studied the market for many years and I'm telling you, Goldie, now's the time to get out."

"I don't have any more stock. Two years ago when you advised me to sell my stock in companies in New York that didn't hire Negroes, I decided to go ahead and sell all the stock I owned. I put the money into federal and state bonds."

"Good move, because pretty soon most stock certificates won't be worth the paper they're printed on. People been borrowing too much to buy all the stock that's being traded lately. Sooner or later, someone is going to have to cough up the money and I don't think all the banks, who have been backing up the stock buyers are going to be able to come up with the money. I paid off the outstanding mortgages on my properties and made arrangements to pre-pay the taxes on all my holdings for the next several years. Invested in federal bonds myself. I don't want you to have to worry about a thing when I'm gone. I just want you to concentrate on your writing."

"You aren't going anywhere anytime soon, Pop."

"Don't matter no way," Pop said before re-lighting his cigar.

All the intricacies of the stock market and the banking industry were foreign to me. My decision to get rid of my stocks was a matter of conscience and convenience. In order to keep up with the stock market, you had to put a lot of time and energy into it. When I decided to sell my stock in Western Union, New York Telephone, and several other New York based companies because of their racist employment policies, I elected to get out of the market altogether. Keeping track of my stock portfolio was taking up too much of my time. Actually, I was quite surprised when my broker mailed me a check for the proceedings from the sale of my portfolio. At first, I thought a mistake had been made, so I immediately telephoned him.

"No mistake has been made Mr. Covington," my broker informed me. "In the past six months, your G.E. stock more than doubled in value, your shares in RCA quadrupled, and most of your utility stocks have also increased drastically."

I knew the price per share of most stocks had been rising on the exchange, but I had no idea they had risen as high and rapidly as they had in three years.

The sounds the tires made as they rolled over the surface of the Brooklyn Bridge alerted me that we were about to cross over into Brooklyn. I felt chilly, so I rolled up the limousine window.

"You back with us now, Goldie?" Herby asked.

"I thought you were napping," Sam added.

"Nah, I was just thinking about the last few conversations I had with Pop. He was convinced that some great evil was about to befall the country. I never could get him to tell me exactly what he meant. He just kept telling me to mark his words, "What goes up eventually must come down."

"He was talking about the stock market. Joseph was convinced that sooner than later, the bottom is going to fall out."

"What do you think, Sam?"

"You know me Goldie. I'm an attorney, not a business whiz like your grandfather was."

"Have you sold any of your stock, Mr. Harris?" Herby asked.

"Sold all my stock. I didn't have any reason to believe that Joseph didn't know what he was talking about. I've trusted his business decisions all my life and I didn't see any reason to stop trusting him then."

Although the ride down Atlantic Avenue to the cemetery near Bushwick and Pennsylvania Avenue seemed to take forever, I didn't mind. It gave me plenty of time to continue reminiscing about Pop.

Pop represented almost 100 years of Negro history. Although he was born a freeman, he was a direct product of the slave trade. He was part of the struggle for the abolition of slavery, both through his participation in the Underground Railroad prior to the Civil War and as a member of the Massachusetts Fifty-fourth during the war. Through his many stories, Pop instilled in me a strong sense of Negro pride. By sharing his memories of the past with me, Pop gave me a strong sense of hope for the future. That sense of hope invoked a feeling in me that I clung to dearly. He used to say, "Unless Negroes believe in their hearts that the future carries with it a promise of better times, then there won't be much of a future for us." He also instilled in me a belief that the future began in the present and you had to continuously work toward making your dreams of the future a reality.

Pop's biggest dream for the future was that one day in America, Negroes would be allowed to share in the American dream on an equal basis with all other Americans, and that the laws of the land would be applied equally to all American citizens, without regard to race, sex, religious beliefs, or national origin.

Although Pop believed that some dark days and troubled times lay ahead for the Negro in America, he believed that one day, perhaps in my lifetime, his dream would become a reality. To that end he worked tirelessly and endlessly. There was no way of measuring how much he contributed to the advancement of our people. I only hoped that I could find a way to contribute a fraction of what he had to the advancement of the quality of life in America for the Negro.

The grave side services took a half hour to complete. The traditional twenty-one gun salute customarily bestowed upon veterans, was touching. Negro veterans from three wars each fired a volley of seven rounds. The veterans of the Civil War were all in their eighties and I suspected that a couple of them were in their nineties. Still, they stood as erect as their aging bodies would allow them and beamed with pride as they paid a final salute to their comrade. The veterans of the Spanish American War, who had stormed San Juan Hill with Teddy Roosevelt, fired the second volley. Herby was one of the World War I veterans who fired the last volley.

After the last of the mourners returned to their cars, I asked Sam and Herby if they wouldn't mind waiting for me in the limousine.

"Tell the driver I'll be there in a few minutes."

"Take your time, champ. No hurry," Sam replied. After giving me a reassuring tap on the shoulder, Sam looked down at Pop's casket and said, "Good-bye, old buddy. I'll be seeing you again one day." I was moved as I watched Sam wipe several tears from his cheek. There was no doubt in my mind; Sam would miss Pop at least as much as I would.

Once I was alone at the grave side, I knelt next to Pop's grave. "Well Pop, I guess this is good-bye. I'm going to miss you, but you'll be with me in my heart every day. Sam thinks that your story should be shared with others. I'm not so sure I'm the one to do it, but I'll give it my best shot. I only wish I had all the old clippings that you saved over the years. It's too bad they burnt up in the fire at your office before I ever got a chance to see them. They sure would have been helpful. I think I can remember enough from the stories you shared with me to do justice to a story of your life. If I can't remember all the details, I'm sure that I could ask Sam to fill me in. Tell you what, if and when I write your biography, I'll come out here and read it to you. Well, I got to go now. I'll drop in on you from time to time."

Before standing, I kissed the palm of my hand and patted the pile of dirt that would soon cover Pop's final resting place on earth. "Good-bye Joseph Cinque Covington," was the last thing I said to Pop before walking away.